GEORGE
WASHINGTON
IS CASH MONEY

GEORGE WASHINGTON IS CASH MONEY

★ ★ ★

A No-Bullshit Guide to the
United Myths of America

★ ★ ★

CORY O'BRIEN

ILLUSTRATED BY SOREN MELVILLE

A PERIGEE BOOK

A PERIGEE BOOK
Published by the Penguin Group
Penguin Group (USA) LLC
375 Hudson Street, New York, New York 10014

USA • Canada • UK • Ireland • Australia • New Zealand • India • South Africa • China

penguin.com

A Penguin Random House Company

GEORGE WASHINGTON IS CASH MONEY

ISBN: 978-0-399-17348-6

This book has been registered with the Library of Congress.

First edition: May 2015

PRINTED IN THE UNITED STATES OF AMERICA

10   9   8   7   6   5   4   3   2   1

To my dad, and the rest of We Tell Stories,
for teaching me and thousands of other kids how
stories are meant to be treated.

OMG, WHAT'S IN THIS BOOK?!

INTRODUCTION

(Or: Emergency Toilet Paper)

'Sup, guys.

One of the things that happened while I was researching this book was that I started reading the introductions to a lot of other books, and I decided maybe my book should have a good introduction too. Introductions are important in books of history and mythology, because they're where authors get a chance to tell you how biased they are.

Me? I'm hella biased. I think the story of the United States is one long, violent soap opera where the best people get killed young and the worst people get rich. But I'm one of the beneficiaries of that story, and the story's not over yet.

See, the other thing I believe is that history and mythology are the same thing. They're stories we dredge out of our pasts in order to make sense of the present, and those types of stories are always going to be necessary. But the stories themselves, and who the main characters are, are always gonna be changing.

Around the turn of the twentieth century, we started a big philosophical movement called the Enlightenment. Thomas Jefferson was a big fan of it, as were a whole grip of scientists and poets and philosophers. The idea was that we were smart enough, technologically advanced enough, to throw off old superstitions and look at the world through the lens of pure reason.

Though these guys were mostly too nervous to say it, Enlightenment philosophy was a pretty big diss to the old concept of religion. Rumor had it that Jefferson was an atheist, but atheism wasn't cool in those days, so if he was, he kept it under his wig. More and more, though, people started to turn to science to answer their questions about the world. And suddenly, the old gods weren't so attractive anymore. "Myth" became a bad word, as you've maybe noticed if you've ever been on Snopes or read a listicle about dumb wrong things people think you should eat.

But when we told the old gods to fuck off, we found ourselves in need of new ones. And no place felt this more than the United States of America. The country is way young, like barely legal, plus the separation of church and state makes it almost impossible to have an official mythology. People need to believe in something, though, so the U.S. has slapped together its own myths, centered around the Founding Fathers, around Science, around The Invisible Hand of the Market. Presidents, gangsters, serial killers, and rock stars are our new pantheon. Politicians invoke the names of Reagan and the Roosevelts. Pop stars are avatars of Marilyn Monroe and Elvis Presley. We put their faces on our money, name our streets after them, erect big stone dicks over their graves. (That last part never changes.)

I've done my best to make the stories in this book as "historically accurate" as possible, but I've also kept a lot of the juicy rumors in, because those are part of history too. Part of the mythology. I've also used some terminology that isn't exactly "politically correct," so let me throw in a quick disclaimer: I know there are other Americas besides the United States of America, and I know the people who originally inhabited the United States part of America were not in fact Indians from India. I'm using these common—if outdated—terms because they fit on the short lines I use, and because sometimes it actually serves to point out the ridiculousness of the terms, *and* because the language I use is a casual, rough, technically incorrect version of English.

Which brings me to why I'm here. I'm here to educate you about the mythology of the United States, the same way we get educated about the mythology of the Greeks and the Romans. Well, not exactly the same way. I've stripped off a lot of the pomp and circumstance. I've added a lot of dick jokes and pop culture references. My friend Soren drew some sweet pictures for you to look at. I guess what I'm saying is that this book is here to educate you about the mythology of the United States the way the Greeks and Romans were educated about theirs, back when *their* shit was new.

TWO STUPID JERKS
INVENT FOOD
(A CHEROKEE CREATION
STORY)

So a long long long long long long long time ago
there was absolutely fuck-all in the entire universe.
Then a little while later, there was some stuff
either because gods made it out of clay and boredom
or just because.
At first all the stuff is underwater
(at least, according to most dudes)
but *Waterworld* is a terrible movie
so all the gods and sassy animals finally wise up
and decide to have land
and some of this land
is a lame-sounding place called Turtle Island.
Wait I mean NORTH AMERICA.
YEEEEEEEEAAAAAAAAA.

But so now there's all this sweet land
and nobody to ruin it.
ENTER: HUMANS.
There are a few theories about how humans entered
like out of the underworld
or from the east
or space
or maybe the gods just had some extra dirt to burn
but WHATEVER
everyone agrees dudes started existing at some point
and that it was a generally bad idea.

Great, so, the universe exists
and there are dudes in it
but riddle me this:
What are these dudes gonna eat?
Don't worry, friends
the Cherokee people got this one covered.

See, shortly after all this world-creating stuff
there's this guy named Kanati.
Kanati has a wife named Selu
and a son named Good Boy
because this is olden times and names are scarce.
Good Boy has a special friend
who hangs out with him by the river
when his parents aren't around.
Good Boy, being a good boy, tells his parents
who are like STRANGER DANGER
and hatch a plan to catch this man.

This is the plan:
The next time Good Boy sees his friend
(whose name is Wild Boy)
he's supposed to "wrestle" him to the ground
and then call his parents
never stopping to consider
that this may be exactly what Wild Boy wants.
Anyway, it happens
and instead of getting registered as a sex offender
Wild Boy gets to live with the rest of the family
as their adopted son
which would be fine
except that Wild Boy is a garbage person.

Let me explain.
Every day, Kanati goes out hunting
and every day he comes home with a ton of meat
and Wild Boy is like "HMM

I WONDER IF I CAN RUIN THIS"
so he takes Good Boy and they go spy on their dad
and it turns out he has this cave
covered with a rock
and when he moves the rock, a deer comes out
like a delicious Easter-time Jesus
and then he shoots that Jesus deer with an arrow
and puts back the rock
and everyone gets deerburgers.

Of course the two boys decide to try this themselves.
This would not be a myth if people didn't suck.
So they go to the cave and move the rock
but they forget to put it back
unleashing a gushing fire hose of woodland fauna
a delicious stampede of totally un-shootable game.
Raccoons and badgers and land-squids and gerbils
and turkeys. Turkeys are VERY IMPORTANT.
But all anyone manages to shoot is one deer's tail
which curls up and that's why deer are all that way.

Anyway, then Kanati shows up like "Aw hell no.
You know what happens when you free the animals?
I'll tell you what happens:
BEEEEEEEES."
So he goes into the back of the cave
and opens up several cans
which might've contained whupass in a different time
but instead contain EVERY KIND OF INSECT
and they're stinging the shit out of these boys
until Kanati decides they've had enough.
Then he's like "Great job, assholes.
Now we have to learn how to actually hunt."

But the boys aren't about to be doing real work
so they go home and ask their mom, Selu, for food
and she's like "We have no food. Because of you.

Assholes."
But they're still her kids, even though they suck
so she goes up to the storeroom to get some grain
and they follow her because they still suck
and they watch her conjure beans and corn
by laying out a bowl and rubbing herself a lot.
So they're like "Holy shit, Mom
are you a witch?"
and she's like "Oh, you think I'm a witch, huh?
Well, how about this:
When I die, drag my clothes around a field seven times
and corn and beans will grow there overnight.
Now who's the witch, huh?"
And the boys are like "Uh, still you."

So Selu dies to spite them
and they half-assedly follow her instructions
like, they only clear a little bit of land
and they only drag her clothes around twice
but they still get corn and beans, so whatever
and then Kanati gets home
from trying to find all the animals
and he's like "Where's my wife?"
and they're like "Oh, you mean Selu?
She turned into a witch and then died"
and Kenati is like "Oh my god, fuck you guys
I'm gonna go live with the wolves."

So he does, and he sends the wolves to kill the boys
but they trap them with magic
and almost drive wolves to extinction
and then they teach everyone how to plant corn
and get reunited with their mom and dad
in the land of the rising sun
but their parents still hate their guts
for many good reasons
so they have to go live on the other side of town
in the bad neighborhood, where the sun sets
but at least they have corn.

All of which just goes to show
that agriculture is for jerks.

They All Laughed at Christopher Columbus . . . Because He Was Dumb

But what's the point of all this sweet land and corn
if it never gets found by any white people?
I'm glad you asked, ethnocentric reader
because it's time for me to tell you the story
of history's number one entrepreneurial sea-jerk.
I refer, of course
to CHRISTOFAR COLOMBO.

Wait shit, that isn't his name.

Well, that's cool
Christopher Columbus isn't his name either.
His real name is something like Crystalballs Colon
and with a name like that
it is shocking to me that he did not end up headlining
at the fourteenth-century equivalent of Chippendales.
Let's just call him Chris.

So Chris is a cheese-merchant's son
who works at his dad's cheese shop
but unlike most sons of cheese merchants at this time
Christopher Columbus has an EXCELLENT PLAN
to make MAD BUXX.
You see Chris lives in Western Europe
and Western Europe is fucking CRAZY about opium
and also whatever else China and Japan sell
like tea and silk and nyan cats

and so far this has not been an issue
because dudes can just walk to China via Russia
buy some shit
and walk back
(it takes kind of a long time but whatever)
but then a bunch of dudes start killing each other
right in the middle of the walking trail
and everyone from Europe is like "Fuck this
I like getting high
but I also like having my organs in my body
but I still REALLY LIKE getting high
we have to find another way into Asia
LET'S USE BOATS."

Most of these people
try to get to Asia by sailing south
around the bottom of Africa
(which is called the horn, mostly for the lols)
and then east
to where Asia is
but Christopher Columbus has a different plan
a fiendishly brilliant plan:
His plan is to sail WEST
AWAY from where Asia is
and then . . . be in Asia.
Now, granted
everyone has known the world is round since Greece
but see the problem
is that China is like twelve thousand miles to the west
a problem that Christopher Columbus solves
by doing his math wrong
and deciding it's about three thousand miles instead.
ALL ABOARD THE SUCCESS TRAIN
WOOO WOOOOOOOOOOOOOOOOOOOO.

Armed with this ambitious and totally legit scheme
Chris does what any modern gentleman would do:

He starts looking for venture capital.
He looks for it in pretty much every court in Europe
which is unfortunate for him
because Europe at this time
seems to be ruled primarily by sane people.
He finally ends up in Spain
where King Ferdinand also says no
and actually offers him big buxx to stay in Spain
either as a court jester
or as a solid to the other kings he would've bugged.
But suddenly, after several years
and a million more identical pitches from Chris
King Ferdinand is like "YOU KNOW WHAT
THIS SUDDENLY SOUNDS AMAZING.
LET'S RIDE THIS FUCKIN' SUCCESS TRAIN
CHUGGA CHUGGA."

Here are the terms that Columbus demands:
1. 10 percent of revenue from any place he discovers
(which is a pretty standard agent rate)
2. Governorship over same lands
3. The title of GREAT ADMIRAL OF THE OCEAN.
Meanwhile, Poseidon rolls in his watery grave.

So Sea King Columbus sets out on his voyage.
He ends up doing four of them
and they go bizarrely fucking well for the guy
like, it turns out there's land
pretty much right where he said it would be
and it's full of people
who sort of look like the people he was looking for
so naturally he calls them Indians
because what else could they be
and then he spends the next decade taxing them
and mutilating the shit out of them when he's bored.
His sons help
it's a bonding experience.

Word gets back to Spain about the mutilating
and in what may be the only recorded instance
of anyone in Europe being nice to natives
they send an investigator to see if the rumors are true
and duh, they are
so they fire Columbus from being governor
and throw him in jail.
This is definitely a grand humanitarian gesture
and not a way to get out of paying Chris his 10 percent
that would be ridiculous.
But Chris's son Diego seems to think that's what's up
so he files a bunch of lawsuits against Spain
which is dumb
because it's hard as shit to sue the government.

Chris does get a couple bucks out of the deal, though
and he also gets to go down in history
as the dude who discovered America
and the dude who discovered that the world is round
and both of those things are totally wrong
but that's okay
because so was Christopher Columbus.

So the moral of the story
is you can get into history the hard way
by being nice to people and right about things
or you can just shoot the moon and be terrible
which seems a hell of a lot easier.

★ ★ ★

The Roanoke Colonists Forget to Leave a Forwarding Address

So Spain's got all these dudes in America now
and England
whose main thing is HATING SPAIN
is like "No way are we gonna sit idly by
while those Spaniards ruin America all by themselves
we gotta get in on this.
First, we need someone as sucky as Chris Columbus.
OH HELLO THERE SIR WALTER RALEIGH."

Sir Walter Raleigh is a government-sponsored pirate
who Queen Elizabeth hires
to SINGLEHANDEDLY COLONIZE AMERICA.
She seriously gives him a permit
that is like "This permit good for one America.
Use it or lose it, buddy."

And use it he does.
He packs a bunch of radical dudes on a boat
and ships them off to an island called Roanoke
off the coast of Virginia
(named after the Queen
whose name is not Virginia, but there you go)
and leaves them there
because he's got better shit to do
than what he was hired to do.

Here's the rub:
There are already other people in Virginia
and they're not friendly!
(Probably because immediately after arriving
the colonists kill an entire tribe
for allegedly stealing a silver cup.
Savages, am I right?
Always stealing cups.)
So the colonists spend 100 percent of their time
fighting off angry natives
and when Raleigh drops by a couple years later
like "Hey, dudes, want a ride home?"
they are like "YES."

So they all leave
a couple days before their reinforcements arrive
and the reinforcements are like "Screw this"
and they go home
but a couple of them have to stay
because remember:
Use it or lose it.
Back in England, Walter Raleigh is like
"I wonder how that colony is doing.
Probably it's doing great.
I should send more dudes to start another colony!"
So he sends another 115 people
including women and children
to this totally safe place.

GUESS WHAT?
NOT ACTUALLY SAFE.

Everybody who stayed behind is now dead.
There's a spooky skeleton and everything
so obviously these new colonists decide to stay
despite the fact that they are super low on food
and surrounded by enemies.

The food thing starts to be a real bummer though
so the governor of the colony
(a dude named John White
because fuck yeah, generic Anglo names)
is like "Okay, guys, I'm gonna run back to England
grab some food and be right back."

THREE YEARS LATER
John White finally comes back with some food
like "OMG, guys, I am so sorry I'm late.
It was winter
and then I got a ride with some pirates
and got captured by the dudes we were trying to rob
and then the Spanish Armada came
and it's just been a really stressful three years so
oh shit where did everybody go?"

Answer: NOBODY KNOWS.
The colonists are all just gone
no spooky skeletons
no houses
no charred remains of houses, even
it's like everybody just packed up and left.

Before John went to England, everybody agreed
that if they got murdered or something
they would carve a cross into a nearby tree
and there is stuff carved into trees
but it is not a cross
it is the word "CROATOA"
which is the name of a nearby island
which John is unable to explore because of a storm
so he just leaves
because mysteries are for chumps.

To this day, nobody agrees what happened
maybe the colonists had sex with the natives

maybe the natives ate the colonists
maybe the colonists were trying to carve a cross
but were just really bad at following directions.
Maybe it was goblins.
Who knows?

Regardless, the moral of the story is the same:
Give a man a fish, and he'll eat for a day.
Abandon a man on a swampy island
a thousand miles from help and home
and he will fucking die.

I Wish
I Could Have
Crashed the First
Thanksgiving

Okay, so there're some extremely Christian dudes.
They're in England and they hate it
I don't blame them
England sucks.
So then they leave in some boats
and they go hit up Amsterdam
because they hear that's where you get the good weed
but then their kids start to do really terrible shit
like learn Dutch
and maybe not be super Christian all the time?
and no amount of good weed is worth that
so they get on some MORE boats
called the *Mayflower* and the *Speedwell*
and they sail to AMERICA
except the *Speedwell* is ironically named
and is actually a slow-as-shit loserbarge
so it has to go home early
and miss the America party.

But it turns out that America is a terrible party
because step one of the party is wait on a boat
forEVER
getting hungry and perpetually seasick
but at least someone poops out a baby
which they name OCEANUS
which is OBJECTIVELY RAD.
But that's the only objectively rad thing in this story

because when they show up in America
it is ULTRA WINTER
like if winter were to take steroids
and then craft for itself a robot ice suit
and team up with Mr. Freeze
to spew catchphrases and ice beams
all over the damn country
that would be about as bad as this winter
AND make for a way better movie.

See they were kind of hoping to find some like
good wholesome Christian white folks
in gated communities
with supermarkets and bowling alleys
but instead they get RUTHLESS WINTER
ALL DAY
ALL THE TIME
ALSO ALL NIGHT
and a ton of people die
because that is the true meaning of winter.

But some people survive the winter
including BRAVE CAPTAIN MILES STANDISH
and he goes out and finds him some Indians
because everyone still sorta thinks they're in India
and one of the Indians is named Squanto
and he's part of the Patuxet tribe
and not a Cherokee at all
but he still somehow knows about corn
so he teaches all the white dudes to plant it
and the white dudes are like "Gee, thanks, Squanto
we will definitely remember this solid you did us
and pay you back in kind forever and ever."

Later, all the crops sprout
and the white dudes go into the forest
and shoot like A THOUSAND turkeys

(see, I TOLD you turkeys were important)
also some deers
(them too!)
and then they cut them all open
and invite EVERYBODY
and all the Indians show up
and bring crazy foreign shit to eat
like potatoes and squash and tomatoes
and everyone is so super jazzed about all this food
that they do not stop partying for THREE DAYS
and there are NINETY DUDES
and HOLY CRAP THAT IS A PARTY
and then the party is over
and the white dudes are like
"Okay, guys, that was great
but we're totally killing you now
you know
for your land."
And the Indians are like "Haha, joke's on you
you can't kill us if we DIE OF SMALLPOX FIRST."
And then everyone decides to relive this occasion
every year
on an arbitrary Thursday
by producing more food
than they can safely consume
and then goading each other into eating it.
Also: families!
But I'm getting ahead of myself.

You see, the real moral of the story
is next time you wanna have a party
but you don't have a good enough reason
maybe just have a party.
Seriously
your reasoning can't be any worse than these dudes'.
(I actually really like Thanksgiving though.)

Salem Sets Ladies on Fire

If I had to use just one sentence to sum up history
it would be:
"People in the past were pretty dumb."
If I had to give an example
it would be the Salem Witch Trials.
Check it out:

All these Puritans are chilling in the New World
with their religious governments
and their no-nonsense clothes
and their chastity and whatever
when all of a sudden this girl starts having seizures
and blaming the woman who does her laundry
and everyone is like "OH NO, WITCHES."

You have to understand that at this time in history
batshit loco was the thing to be
people had been believing in magic since forever
and they weren't about to stop
but they HAD all decided that magic was evil
so they were definitely willing to kill any damn lady
who was acting sort of witchy.

Luckily for the washer lady
there's this dude named Cotton Mather
who decides to cure this twitching child
by bringing her over to his house
and praying at her until she stops spazzing
and I guess Cotton Mather's house is so crazy boring
that the chick sobers up real fast

and that's the end of that problem.
NOT.
Because now children all over Massachusetts
know that seizures are a great way to get attention
so these two girls over in Salem Village
(not to be confused with Salem Town
which is right next door
and also part of this story
just to confuse you)
start flipping the literal hell out
all screaming, yelling, crawling under furniture
you know
THE KIND OF DUMB SHIT KIDS DO
and when everyone is like "Stop being shitty!"
They're like "We can't because witches."

So in an effort to get their children to shut up
the people of Salem arrest a homeless lady
an independent woman
and a slave named Tituba
who is too foreign and interesting to live
and this would all be fine
except that when you get arrested for witchcraft
the first thing they ask you is
"Hey, do you know any other witches?
Maybe we will go easy on you if you tell us."
SO WHAT DO YOU THINK HAPPENS?

I'll tell you.
What started out as a childish prank
rapidly becomes an unstoppable snowball of murder.
The more witches they arrest
the more witches those witches tell them about
and the more children start having freaky seizures
and blaming random people they don't like.
And instead of being like "Oh damn
so many hangings

maybe we should slow down and do less hanging"
the people of Salem are like "OH DAMN
SO MANY WITCHES
BETTER RELAX OUR JUDICIAL STANDARDS."

At this point it becomes legal to convict a person
based solely on what is called "spectral evidence."
Here is what spectral evidence is:
Let's say I don't like you
because you cut in front of me at the Burger Barn
so I go to the Court of Oyer and Terminer in Salem
and I say, "Hey, last night I was in bed
and the spirit of Asshole McGee over there
[we're assuming that's your name
just for the sake of example]
flies into my room and starts punching my dick
OBVIOUSLY A WITCH."
YOU WOULD BE CONVICTED FOR THAT.

So now people are dying like flies in a blender
like, they kill a dude named Giles Cory
by stacking rocks on top of him until he dies
because he WON'T ADMIT TO BEING A WITCH
and they hang this lady Mary Easty
who is like SUPER pious
and keeps being like "Guys, I actually didn't do this!"
(although later the government feels bad
and pays her family like two thousand bucks
so all is forgiven)
and Cotton Mather is like "Hey, guys?
You know, witches are real bad and all
but maybe chill out a bit?"
And everyone's like "WHAT'S THAT YOU SAY?
WITCHES ARE BAD?
YES, WE KNOW
THAT IS WHY WE'RE KILLING SO MANY."
and Cotton Mather is like *shrug*

But finally, shit gets out of hand.
Now, I know what you're thinking
you're thinking: Shit was already out of hand
it was nowhere near the hand
like here's the hand
and here's Egypt
and then over here
in an anonymous hovel in the Gobi desert
is where you might find the shit.
And you're right
but it was okay up to this point
because the only people getting killed were poor.
After a while though
people just start accusing absolutely anybody
and one of those people is the governor's wife
and the governor is like "Whoa, whoa, hey
maybe we're being a little hasty, guys
how about we uh . . . stop killing witches.
Yeah, you know what?
Pardons for everybody!
Yayyyy!"
Meanwhile twenty people have been executed
and five have died in prison.

So the moral of the story
is that children are assholes.

* ★ ★

Tea Is for Wankers

So there's these dudes in America
and the reason I am calling it America
as opposed to the United States thereof
is because these states are in no way united
they are about as cohesive a legislative body
as a shot glass full of sperm.
But that's all about to change
because one thing these dudes DO agree on
is they really don't like England
specifically the king of England
whose name is George The Third
which just shows how unfit for command he is.
What kind of king lets himself be named George?
If I was king
I would be named Hugedick Excelsior
THE FIRST
BECAUSE APPARENTLY
NO ONE ELSE THINKS OF THIS STUFF.

But oh, I should explain why George is a tool
and in order to do that
we gotta get knee-deep in that most British of fluids
that's right
TEA
(I think every country has an official fluid
like France has wine
and Russia has vodka
and Greenland has tears).

Believe it or not, the British did not invent tea
they just kinda invented putting tea on boats
that got it from Asia
along with every other cool thing.
The reason this is important
is that there is only one company in Britain
that is allowed to import tea
and that company is known as
THE BRITISH EAST INDIA COMPANY
(which I will from now on refer to
as the Notorious E.I.C.).

But it's not that simple.
See, Britain charges a pretty hefty tax on that tea
and then the EIC sells it to other dudes
who sell THAT tea to colonists in America
who have to pay ANOTHER tax on that tea
and aren't allowed to buy tea from anyone else
all of which adds up to SUPER EXPENSIVE TEA
which is just like
what the fuck
you're already drinking fucking tea
and now it's EXPENSIVE too?
Fuck tea
drink 40s.

But the colonists are desperate for shitty leaf-water
so they start buying it off of Dutch smugglers
for like half the price
and also raising hell about the stupid tea tax.
They're like, "Listen, guys
we didn't vote for your stupid government
so stop making us pay money to it.
We don't come into your parliament
and slap the dumb powdered wigs off your heads
so stop telling us how much to pay for tea.

FUCK TEA

SHOVE IT TO THE B.I.C.

an *EFFECTIVE SPECIFIC* for the *Treatment* of *BRITISH IMPERIALISM*

DRINK 40's

endors'd by the Sons of Liberty

Haha, 'to pay' kinda sounds like 'toupee'
which is basically what those wigs are.
Seriously you guys look like assholes."

Naturally Britain is pretty peeved
but the colonies are rich and have guns
so Britain decides to repeal all their recent taxes
EXCEPT the tea law
because fuck you, America.
This kind of defeats the purpose of the repeal
but they do manage to lower the price of tea
until it's ONE CENT cheaper than Dutch
    tea
which . . . I mean . . . just repeal the tax, seriously.

So a bunch of colonists get together
who call themselves the Sons of Liberty
and they're like "You know what
tea is actually pretty gross
this was never about tea
this was actually about fuck you."

Meanwhile, the EIC is bringing a huge load of tea
so the Sons of Liberty get together
and go around scaring the crap out of tea importers
to get them to send the ships back
and they are apparently really scary
'cause everybody they talk to agrees to do it
EXCEPT IN MASSACHUSETTS.

Massachusetts has this governor, you see
his name is Thomas Hutchinson
and he is a tea-loving, British-sympathizing douche
whose sons run most of the tea-importing in Boston.
So as far as he's concerned
that shit is getting IMPORTED.

Enter Sam "Samuel" Adams
he's a Bostonian rabble-rouser
who brews his own beer
and is completely furious about this tea thing
so basically
this is a dude who just likes to get fucked up
(or who doesn't like taxation without representation
whatever, same diff).
Sammy calls a meeting
and a bunch of Sons of Liberty show up
and they're like "Hey, boat guys
you better not unload all that tea!"
and Thomas Hutchinson is like "Hey, boat guys
you better unload all that tea!"
and the boat guys are like "Aaa, aaaa
we are so confused and more boats keep showing up
what do we do???"
and Sam Adams is like "I dunno guys
I guess it's out of my hands.
WINK."

And then BAM
a bunch of dudes in Indian costumes
(because yes
that's apparently still where they think they are)
are all over those boats
whooping and yelling and chucking tea into the water
thus cementing the American preference for coffee
while simultaneously inventing the rager
and all the boat guys are like "Phew"
and eventually an ultraconservative party
names itself after this event
but it's a political party, not a fun party
and they don't throw any tea in the water
so all they get out of the association
is the ability to make "tea-bagging" jokes
which is really more of a net win for their enemies.

So the moral of the story
is if you are having trouble deciding
between two equally shitty options
there is always a third option:
throw everything in the ocean.

★ ★ ★

THE DECLARATION OF INDEPENDENCE, OR: MUCH ADO ABOUT FREEDOM

Now, if there's one thing that pisses off Brits
it's wasting their tea
so when the Sons of Liberty dump it all in the bay
King George and Co. get mighty angry
and in a stunning display of passive-aggressiveness
they pass a bunch MORE terrible laws:

1. The port of Boston is now closed
2. Massachusetts doesn't get a government
3. Royal employees basically can't go to jail
4. British soldiers can sleep in your house
and finally, the most terrible provision of all:
5. CANADA GETS MORE LAND.

Now, as we all know
hatred for Canada is a proud American tradition
(except when you don't like who the president is
or you're on the run from the cops
or you need health care)
so naturally the colonists gotta do something
and do something they do
. . . eventually.

Remember when I said everyone agrees
about how King George is a dick?
I lied. Not everyone agrees.

No one agrees on anything.
That is the secret of America.
But there are some dudes who are mad eager
to MAKE everyone agree.
One of them is named John Adams
(the less sexy brother of Sam Adams)
and he is so gung ho about independence
that he is prepared to go to WAR for it.
But before he goes to real war for it
he has to go to POLITICAL war
which is like real war
except less like real war
and more like planning a party
where all the guests hate each other.

So think of it like this:
Adams and some of his bros
(that is, Tom Jefferson and Ben Franklin)
are planning a rager called the Continental Congress
(exactly as sexy as it sounds).
They invite everybody they know
because if they don't invite someone
it's just gonna be a whole lot of drama
and meanwhile, the cops
(that is, the British Empire)
are on their way to SHUT THIS PARTY DOWN
so dudes gotta move fast if they wanna get drunk
(that is, establish a fair and independent government).

So delegates from all these colonies show up
and pack their sweaty bodies into a single room
in the middle of summer
to try to compose a sensitive political document
and SURPRISE, SURPRISE, they start fighting.
Pennsylvania and Maryland are like "Naw, dudes
no way are we going independent"
and New York is like "Seriously, guys

I would love to vote for independence
but my government won't let me"
and John Adams is like "Don't be weenies
tell your parents/governments/constituents
to just piss off"
and Maryland and Pennsylvania are like "Make us"
and John Hancock is like "Whoa, guys, calm down!"
(Hancock is president of the Continental Congress
which really just means he sits in a big chair
and tells everyone to calm down.)

So Adams is like "Okay, how about this:
We don't declare independence tonight
but I write a REALLY mean letter
about how we're GONNA declare independence
eventually."
And Pennsylvania is like "Fine whatever,"
but Maryland just says "Fuck this" and leaves.

But John Adams won't be so easily discouraged.
He grabs a bunch of his brother's good beer
rolls up his ridiculous pantaloons
and starts sending out another round of invites.
So everyone shows up
because the last party sucked
but at least it's something to do
and GUESS WHAT?
EVERYBODY'S STILL BICKERING.
Pennsylvania is all "Aaaa, I dunno
maybe we should invite France first
in case shit gets nasty with the cops"
and John Adams is like "Dudes:
Right now, this party we're having
we're kinda throwing it at our parents' house
like, while they're out of town
France is not gonna show up for that shit
France is way too cool for that
we need to be able to tell them it's OUR house
then we can have rad parties all the time
and pay whatever we want for tea."
and Pennsylvania is like "Well
my royal government just exploded, so I'm in"
and Maryland is like "Okay, fiiiiiine"
and New York is like "Guys, I'd really love to
but I have to talk to my government first
and they're out of town right now
and they won't be back for like a month"
so everyone else is like "Wow, you're such a baby.
Fine, we'll vote without you."

Thus commences the party-within-a-party
known as the "Committee of Five."
As the name implies, it has five dudes
but only three that history really cares about:
Ben "Big Dick" Franklin
Thomas "Violent J" Jefferson

and John "Not Samuel" Adams.
Everyone wants Adams to write the Declaration
but he's like "Naw, get Jefferson to do it
I'm tired of revolutionizing America for a bit."

So Jefferson throws something together
in like two weeks
and everyone agrees that it sort of sucks
so they revise the hell out of it
which TJ doesn't like because he's a little diva.
The final version looks something like this:

THE DECLARATION OF INDEPENDENCE
AHEM:
Y'ALL ARE BEING DICKS
AND YOU DON'T SEEM TO WANT TO STOP
SO WE OUT.

SINCERELY,
JOHN HANCOCK
(and a bunch of other dudes with smaller names)

So yeah, after all that shit John Adams did
the biggest and sexiest name on the Declaration
belongs to some rando dude
whose only historical achievement
is signing his name real big
which just goes to show
that if all you want is to be remembered forever
calligraphy is way easier to learn than politics.

★ ★ ★

GEORGE WASHINGTON IS
CASH MONEY

If you like America
then you probably love this next dude
(if you don't like America, then wow
why did you buy this book)
this is the dude who invented being president
the dude who is literally money
the dude who has more monuments dedicated to him
than he has real teeth.
Yes friends
I am talking about George Washington:
AMERICA'S DAD.

George is born back in colonial times
to a pretty rich family of planters in Virginia
and from the moment this kid is born
he just gives ZERO fucks.
Like one time he sees a cherry tree
and he's like "FUCK THAT TREE"
and he chops it down
for no better reason than he has an axe that can do it
and then his dad is like "WHO DID THAT?!"
and George is like "ME.
WHATCHA GONNA DO?"
Some people say that didn't actually happen
but even if it didn't
it's the sort of thing he would do.

But George is more than just an axe-swinging maniac
he is also really, really tall

33

taller than everyone
(people were hella short in the past
so this was not hard)
and the British take one look at this tall son of a bitch
and they're like "MY WORD
LET'S MAKE THE BIG FELLOW A GENERAL."

So George ends up commanding a thousand dudes
during the French and Indian War
which is basically over who gets Ohio.
He's an okay general
his guys are pretty disciplined
except once
they accidentally shoot sixteen British dudes
so that's embarrassing.
Which is prolly why George doesn't stay a general.
After the war, he goes back to just being wealthy
and owning slaves and marrying for money.
You know, the American way.
And he gets mad rich this way
just growing plants out of the ground
and selling them to dudes who put them on boats
which is probably why
when the British start imposing all these crazy taxes
on things that come and go on boats
George is like "NUH UH."

The cool thing about being a rich landowner
is that you don't really have to do work
so you are free to show up to every political meeting
and make your opinions on taxes heard
so when the Continental Congresses start happening
George is all up in there
wearing a military uniform
to let everyone know he is ready to kill for cheap tea
and since pretty much everyone at the meeting

has been over to his house for dinner at some point
for sweet rich-people-only parties
(plus they're all Freemasons together)
they're all pretty much on the same page.

So when Paul Revere shows up
like "THE BRITISH ALL UP INS"
everyone looks at George Washington
and he's like "... What?
Why is everybody looking at me?
Oh, you want me to lead your army?
Okay, fine."

George has been itching to lead an army
ever since his so-so performance under the Brits
so he pulls out all the stops.
He's recruiting soldiers from everywhere
he's lobbying the states for more troops and money
and he's retreating
a lot.

See, even with George Washington's pull
the Continental Army is WAY smaller than Britain's
which means George's strategy boils down to:
"Make it LOOK like we have a fighting army
long enough to convince France we're winning
so they come over to help fuck the British
and then we can just have them win the war for us."

This is further complicated by the fact
that Washington's troops are constantly dying
not from war
(I mean, that helps)
but from not getting their smallpox vaccines
and the ones who don't die just wait a few months
and then peace out when their contracts run out

and Washington is like "AUGH, GUYS
WHAT DO I HAVE TO DO
TO GET YOU TO DIE FOR YOUR COUNTRY?"

It turns out all he has to do
is bully Congress into passing Draconian laws
punishing deserters and lengthening service contracts
plus then France starts helping out
(yes, the same France he fought in that other war)
so in between vaccinating his troops
and murdering British-allied Indian tribes
(some of whom he negotiated the alliances with)
he manages to turn the war around
and despite his soldiers being pretty sucky
he finally routs the British single-handed!
(except for a huge French fleet
and a lot of French money
but you know, whatever).

Then the war is over
and all the soldiers are like "SHIT YEAH, GEORGE
COME BE OUR KING."
and George is like "Um, no
we just fought a war against King George
and there can't be two King Georges at once
that would be confusing."
So he disbands his whole army
LIKE AN IDIOT
and then shows up to the Constitutional Convention
and doesn't even talk or anything
just sits there looking regal and paternal
until everyone is like "UGH FINE
YOU CAN BE PRESIDENT, GOD
NOT LIKE ANYONE ELSE IS EVEN RUNNING.
Well, other than John Adams
but what did he do?
Other than draft the Declaration of Independence

and take an active role in framing the Constitution?
Seriously, fuck that guy
have you met his brother Sam?
So much cooler."

George is actually a pretty good president.
His main job is to not be a dick
so that future presidents also refrain from dickery
but after eight years he gets sick of being righteous
and resigns
and goes back to his farm to be rich until he dies
at which point he frees his slaves
sorry, most of his slaves
dude has a lot of slaves
you can't expect him to just free all of them
that would be almost human.

Then he dies
and everyone argues over where to stuff his corpse
like, in Virginia
or in the capital city WHICH BEARS HIS NAME
(much the way Athens bears Athena's, coincidentally)
but they settle on Virginia
so as not to piss off the South
and try to make up for it by carving his face in a hill
and building him a giant stone dick in the capital
and painting pictures of him
and naming another state after him
and basically every street in every city
and putting him on half the money
all of which just goes to show
that traditionally
the president of the United States
is the guy in the group
who is the most excited about shooting other guys.

★ ★ ★

Rip Van Winkle Sleeps His Way to the Top

Now, I've been talking a lot about rich dudes
and what they were doing during the revolution
but what about poor dudes?
What were they doing?
Well, according to this pack of fictional lies
they were SLEEPING.
Listen:

There's this dude named Rip Van Winkle
he's a pretty decent bro
always mowing his neighbors' lawns
fixing their roofs
drinking their booze
but see the problem with Rip Van Winkle
is that he is only capable of doing things
that IN NO WAY BENEFIT HIM
like, he can't mow his own lawn
he can't fix his own roof
and he'd probably drink his own booze
except he can't afford any
BECAUSE HE HAS NO JOB
so mainly he just wanders around town
with his dog named Wolf
which is a shitty name for a dog
but probably an even shittier name for a wolf
unless it's Wolf from Star Fox
but I think he's called Star Wolf
or am I making that up?
If I am, and that name isn't taken
I am hereby changing my name to Star Wolf.

ANYWAY
Rip Van Winkle has a wife
I forget what her name is
so we will just call her Bitchingstein Don Crunk
because this woman is currently working on her MA
in applied bitchology
all like "BLUH BLUH BLUH
WHY DON'T YOU GET A JOB
SO WE CAN FEED OUR CHILDREN
AND/OR NOT BE THE LAUGHINGSTOCK
OF THE ENTIRE NEIGHBORHOOD"
It's like she wants him to contribute to the household
instead of just drinking booze and leeching off her.
What a bitch, am I right?
But Rip isn't fazed by her henpeckery.
One day he is just like "You know what
I don't have to listen to this
I'm gonna go wander around with my dog
IN THE WOODS."

So he's wandering around in the woods
and he sees this dude
struggling uphill with a BIG BARREL OF BOOZE
and Rip is like "Hey, buddy
that booze looks pretty heavy
maybe I ought to help you carry it
WITH MY MOUTH
or I guess I could just use my hands."

So they carry the keg to the top of the mountain
where there is this cave
and inside the cave
there are a bunch of weird tiny fellas
just hanging out
bowling
and no one is saying anything
so Rip is just like "Okay, guys

I'm just gonna take position right next to this booze
and drink myself senseless.
Please continue bowling to indicate your assent."
And they keep bowling
and Rip Van Winkle drinks until he blacks out
and the gnomes draw dicks on him with a Sharpie.

When he wakes up
he's got like a ten-foot beard
and his hunting rifle has rusted away
and his dog is missing

(fun fact: his dog is actually dead)
and he is like "Daaaaang
I think I might have had too much to drink.
Oh well, time to go back to my ordinary life."
So he goes back to town
and he doesn't recognize a SINGLE PERSON
and everyone is like "Who the hell are you?"
and he is like "I'm a loyal subject of England
just like you guys!"
and everyone is like "WRONG MOVE, ROYALIST."

See, Rip's been asleep for TWENTY YEARS
and in that time the American Revolution happened
so people are no longer down with King George
they are down with George Washington
and there is only room for one George in their lives
but really it doesn't matter at all
and pretty soon everyone stops giving a shit
and Rip moves in with his daughter
who is now conveniently old enough
for him to leech off of
and he finds another dog
and he basically goes back
to doing exactly what he was doing before he left
with the added bonus that now his wife is dead

This story reveals a potent little life hack:
If everyone is yelling at you for being irresponsible
try being MORE irresponsible
and maybe they will all die while you are in a coma.

★ ★ ★

BENJAMIN FRANKLIN IS
THE GOD OF LIGHTNING

I know what you're expecting
because I know how books like this usually go.
I'm supposed to tick off the Founding Fathers
one by one
and tell you what assholes they all actually are.
You know why popular history likes to do this?
Because everyone loves to see their heroes look bad
and if you have enough information about a dude
it is SUPER EASY to make him look like a dingus.
BAM
INSTANT BESTSELLER.

I did it with Christopher Columbus
because he's terrible
and I did it with George Washington
'cause he's the colonial equivalent of a trust fund kid
but now it's time to talk about Ben Franklin
and I won't do it.
It's not that I can't make Big Ben look like a prick.
Dude may have (definitely) hit on his best bro's girl
while his bro was out of town one time
and he may have (definitely) refused to marry a lady
because her parents wouldn't pay off ALL HIS DEBT
and he may have (definitely) cheated on his wife
and then fathered a son
who eventually fought against him in the revolution
but when the best dirt historians can dig up on you
is that you had a lot of extramarital sex
well, at worst
you're the Zeus of the thirteen colonies.

Ben gets born in Boston around 1706
which means he had exactly seventy years
to become enough of a ruckus-causer
to spark off the American Revolution.
Yeah
imagine your granddad banging hookers in France
while simultaneously negotiating military treaties
and maybe then you'll understand why I like this guy.

Anyway he gets born
he works for his brother as a printer for a while
teaches himself writing
(because he's too poor for college)
and then goes "fuck this" and moves to Philly
because he hears they have dope sandwiches.
In Philly, he keeps being a printer
and he's so goddamn good at it
(spoiler: Ben Franklin is good at EVERYTHING)
that pretty soon
dudes are just handing him cash to buy his own press
and start his own business.

So now he becomes a master printer
buys a couple slaves
(but don't worry, he frees them later
and he doesn't even have to die first!)
and starts a newspaper
which he uses to manipulate the opinions
of Philadelphia's ENTIRE GOVERNMENT.
He also starts a weekly discussion group
which gets so popular
that each member starts his own discussion group
and from that point on
Ben Franklin owns Philadelphia.

Let me explain how this works:
Anytime Benjamin Franklin wants a thing to happen

the first thing he does is write a paper about it
then he reads it in his discussion group
and then he gives it to each of his members
and has them read it in *their* discussion group
then he publishes it in his newspaper
which is the most popular newspaper in the city
and then when everybody is talking about his plan
he goes to the assembly
(which he is also the clerk of, coincidentally)
and is like "Hey, guys
it seems like everybody wants this thing to happen
maybe you should do it."
BOOM. POLITICS.

He uses this technique to get a night watch
a fire department
a militia
a hospital
a university
paved roads
and a library
(while also securing himself a contract
to print ALL THE MONEY IN PENNSYLVANIA).
You couldn't throw a rock down a street
without hitting a public service attributable to him
and even if you did
your rock would be quickly swept up
by the street sweepers Franklin employed.

So obviously he becomes unreasonably wealthy
and he tries to retire
but everyone is like "NOPE
YOU HAVE TO BE IN THE ASSEMBLY NOW"
and he's like "Aw man, really?
I was looking forward to a life of leisure
just doin' science and hot chicks forever."
But he does it anyway.

Then when shit starts getting crazy in the colonies
he goes to England
and he's like "Guys, maybe we should make a deal
where you don't act like you can make laws for us
and we maybe don't kill all your guys"
and the British are like "PISH POSH"
and Ben's like "Okay
maybe stop being British for a sec
and just listen to me"
and the British are like "BALDERDASH"
and Ben is like "Okay, well
I guess I'm gonna go tell France to kill you now"
and the French
(who at this time in history
will take ANY opportunity to screw with England)
are like *"OUI OUI"*
and Ben is like "God dammit
I'm surrounded by foreigners."

But Franklin is not content
simply to challenge the British Empire
he has to challenge THE GODS THEMSELVES
specifically Zeus, god of lightning
presumably because he didn't like the competition
when it came to illegitimate sexytimes.

So Ben decides to find out what's up with electricity
which means he has to take a break
from single-handedly inventing Philadelphia
to run some experiments
and it turns out that there is one particular experiment
that everyone else is too much of a weenie to run
and that is the experiment
that will finally answer the age-old question:
"IS LIGHTNING MADE OF ELECTRICITY????"
COME ON
COME THE FUCK ON

IT'S *LIGHTNING*.
WHEN YOU GET HIT BY LIGHTNING
IT GOES BZZT
AND YOUR SKIN GOES TRANSPARENT
AND EVERYONE CAN SEE YOUR BONES
HOW IS THIS NOT OBVIOUS?
Man, the past is dumb.

But Big Ben Franklin is NOT
so he does the smartest possible thing
which is to make a kite out of metal and silk
attach a key to the bottom
and go out in a lightning storm.
This guy is on our money, America.
Not only is he on our money
he's on a denomination of money
that I'm not even rich enough to possess.
Anyway, this experiment is a great success
Benjamin Franklin finally proves
that lightning is the only thing it could possibly be
and he writes a paper about it
and sends it to the Royal Society of London
and they're all like "POPPYCOCK!
LIGHTING IS MADE OF GLOWING BEES
EVERYONE KNOWS THAT."
And they refuse to acknowledge the experiment
until some French dudes run it better.

This brings to mind an old adage:
Early to bed
and early to rise
will not make you as cool
as Benjamin Franklin.
SLEEP LATE HAVE SEX.

★ ★ ★

ALEXANDER HAMILTON IS
A STRAIGHT-UP G

I am not even kidding about this.
Let's start from the beginning.
Dude is born in the West Indies
and by the time he is eleven years old
he is already an orphan
but instead of pulling some Oliver Twist shit
and turning to crime and eating soup or whatever
he just impresses the pants off all these adults
with how smart he is
and then he's like "Hey, guys
since your pants are all around your ankles
why don't you bend down
fish your wallets out of your pockets
and fund my trip to a North American college?"
and all the adults are like "Wow, okay
thought that was going somewhere WAY different."

So Alex goes to America
which isn't even really America yet
just a collection of sassy colonies
and then the revolution happens and everything
but that's not enough for li'l Hammy
because the colonies are independent now
but they're only bound together
by these weak-ass Articles of Confederation
that basically say, "Yeah, we're a country I guess
but like
whatever
do what you want."

So Alex and some other dudes
who call themselves the Federalists
decide they REALLY need a strong constitution
that gives the central government ACTUAL powers
and in order to convince people to do this
Alex and his bros write like eighty essays about it
and Alex alone writes FIFTY of those essays.
FIFTY essays
that's like twice the number of essays
I DIDN'T write in college.
Alexander Hamilton don't play.

So the constitution gets signed
and dudes are pleased.
Then when his bro John Adams becomes president
Hammykins is suddenly a top political dude
so he's like "Hey, guys, you know what we need?
A CENTRAL BANK."
And the Democratic-Republicans
(which is a mega clunky name
for dudes who hate them some Federalists)
are like "NO WAY"
and Alex is like "YES WAY" and does it anyway.
So let's review:
streets of the West Indies
to founder of the first Federal Bank.
If anybody deserves to be on money
it's this dude.

But for every straight-up G
there is the inevitable beef
and for Alexander Hamilton
the name of that beef is Aaron Burr.
When it comes to beef
what these two dudes have is some wagyu shit.
I'm talking grass-fed
free-range

hand-massaged
HATRED.
Like, when Aaron Burr is tied to be president
Alexander Hamilton makes sure he's vice president.
Then, when Aaron Burr runs for New York
    governor
Alexander Hamilton makes sure he's NOTHING
and the way he accomplishes this
is by talking endless smack about Aaron Burr
at like every party he goes to
which means word is BOUND to get around.

So Aaron hears about this
and he hits up Alex like "Yo, Hamilton
you been talking smack about me?"
and Hamilton's like "I do talk smack, sir"
and Aaron is like "But do you talk smack about me?"
and Hamilton is like "I DO TALK SMACK, SIR"
and Aaron's like "Okay, that's it.
I have to shoot you now."
And Hamilton is like "Yeah, I guess you're right
this is the world we live in."
THIS IS THE WORLD THEY LIVE IN.

So these bros murder-elope to New Jersey
where dueling is SLIGHTLY LESS ILLEGAL
and they stand across from each other
and then Alex shoots his gun into the air
and Aaron shoots his gun into Alex's organs
and Alex is like "Oh dang
probably should have pointed my gun at that guy."
and then he dies.
Now, some people say Hamilton meant to miss
and some say that's just a thing he told people
to make himself look good in case he shot wrong
but one thing is certain:
HAMILTON SHOT FIRST.

This was not an isolated incident, my friends.
I mean, Hamilton himself
was in TEN OTHER DUELS before this one
and the place where he got shot
hosted HUNDREDS of other duels
between trigger-happy assclowns
who had insulted each other at the theater
or splashed mud on each other from a carriage
or whatever other unforgivable insult
makes it okay to meticulously schedule a murder
just to preserve your self-esteem
and you know who did this more than anyone?
GOVERNMENT PEOPLE.
GO FIGURE.

Anyway, to this day
the guns that were used in that duel
are proudly displayed
at the headquarters of Chase Manhattan Bank
which is close enough to a temple, I guess
especially considering Hamilton's whole bank thing.

Why tell you this story, dear reader?
To prove to you the simple truth
that politics
used to be WAY more satisfying.

THOMAS JEFFERSON IS A RADICAL MAN, BUYING RADICAL LAND

So George Washington gets to be president
it's pretty cool
then he stops being president
which is even cooler
because he could have done it forever if he wanted
and it takes a pretty rad guy to give that all up.
But then everyone's like "Aw snap
now we actually have to do that thing we said
where we peacefully transfer power to a new leader
ughhhhhhh
why can't we just elect another godlike war hero?"
but no one can live up to G. Washington
so everyone is just like fuck it
and they elect John Adams
(who was George's vice president)
as president
and Thomas Jefferson
(who fucking hates John Adams)
as vice president.

You see, back in the day
you didn't get to pick your running mate
the vice presidency just went to the dude
who everybody liked the second most
and there are plenty of reasons
to like Thomas Jefferson the second most.
First of all, he LOVES revolutions
and everyone in America kinda does too

considering they just did one.
In fact, TJ is the (literally) radical dude
who wrote the first draft of the Declaration
and then got all pissy when people changed it
so he is even revolutionary among revolutionaries.
He's also a fan of the Bill of Rights
(which is basically like the Ten Commandments
except it's for governments instead of people
and there's nothing in it about the Sabbath
and banging your neighbor's wife is totally okay).
Also, Jefferson is tall
which counts for a lot in American politics.

But there's also plenty to hate about Jefferson
especially if you're John Adams.
See, John Adams is a big fan of England
with its tea
and its venerable monarchy
and Jefferson is a big fan of France
with its republican revolution
and its constant war with England.
John Adams is a fan of a strong central government
Jefferson thinks bloody local uprisings are
    hilarious
John Adams wants a central bank
Jefferson fucks his friends' wives.
They're like two wackily mismatched roommates
in the sitcom that shaped their entire country.

So while Adams tries to be a good president
Jefferson fucks off to his Virginia mansion
which is such a baller crib
that there's a picture of it ON OUR MONEY
and when John Adams is done taking the blame
for literally every bad thing that happens
in the four years he is president
Jefferson shows up and is like "Hey, guys

vote for me
I am so much more radical than this guy."

He gets elected pretty hard
and his vice president ends up being Aaron Burr
who is a shitty jerk who sucks
and goes on to murder Alexander Hamilton
(the founder of the first national bank)
and after that
everyone is like "Okay
maybe we should get to pick our own running mates."

But anyway
when Jefferson becomes president
he suddenly gets WAY LESS RADICAL
well, okay, he stays kind of radical
but instead of using his radicalism
to undermine government powers at every turn
he uses his government powers
to just do crazy shit without asking anyone if it's okay.
Like there are these Turkish sultans
and they are kidnapping American sailors
so Jefferson takes the navy
(which he told John Adams not to build)
sends it all to the Mediterranean
and then a week or so later
after it's too late to do anything about it
he's like "Hey, Congress
totally declared a war just now
oh, and look at that
looks like I just won it too.
How do you feel about that?"
and Congress is like "Oh, you."

Also, he's been banging one of his slaves
this WHOLE TIME.
He frees all the children they have

and he's not technically cheating on his wife
since his wife is dead
and he does start paying her a salary
instead of just making her work for free
so he's really not even banging his slave
he's just banging his EMPLOYEE
WHO HE ALSO SORT OF OWNS.
This from the dude behind the Bill of Rights.
Nice, dog.
Nice.

But Jefferson is more than just a sex criminal
He's also REALLY SUPER GREEDY.
See, America is fine right now
but the problem with it
is that it's only slightly huge
and Jefferson wants to supersize that shit.
At this time, Spain owns a ton of land
out to the west of where the colonies are.
They haven't even explored that shit
they just showed up and decided they owned it
it's an awesome trick
you should try it some time.
But then Napoleon takes over France
(so much for republicanism)
and makes an alliance with Spain
and part of the alliance is
"I get to act like I own all that land in America."
So Jefferson goes to Napoleon
and he's like "Hey, bro
I hear you have a bunch of land.
I'm willing to give you a couple bucks for some of it"
and Napoleon
who is fighting wars with like everybody
and really needs money to keep doing that
is like "Sure, dude, take all of it
whatever, it's not even really mine

I don't know what's in it or anything
and neither do you, so I dunno why you want it
but whatever, go nuts."

This purchase straight-up DOUBLES U.S. territory
and it costs like four cents an acre.
It's like if you had a house
and you went over to your neighbor's house
and you were like "Hey, bra
kinda want your house
I will give you half of this old burrito for it"
and he was like "HELL YEAH
DO YOU WANT MY SWIMMING POOL TOO?"

So naturally everybody thinks Jefferson's the shit
even though he had to use the central bank to do this
and he was originally opposed to the bank.
Whatever, land trumps morals
AS WE WILL LEARN AGAIN AND AGAIN.
His second term in office is hella boring though
and then later he retires
and even later he dies
on the FOURTH OF JULY
the same day as John Adams
who is so embarrassed about all the shit he gave him
that his last words are pretty much "Oh man
I wonder what Thomas Jefferson is up to."
But you know what doesn't retire or die?
DAT LAND.

I think we can all learn a valuable lesson from this:
If folks are about to discover what a jerk you are
distract them with a large chunk of unmapped forest.

★ ★ ★

Lewis and Clark: The New Adventures of Superman . . . No, Wait

So there are these dudes
Meriwether Lewis and Dan Clark or whatever
everyone just calls them by their last names
and then Thomas Jefferson is like "Guys
hey, guys
I just bought all this land from Napoleon
like way more than I need.
I have no idea what's in it
could you guys go find out for me?
I will give you basically as much money as you want
plus
you will be FAAAAMOUS."

He actually says this to Lewis first
because Lewis is a proven badass
who fought in wars and stuff
but Lewis knows he's a loose cannon
so he's like "Can I bring my bro Clark?
He's way chiller than me.
He would be an ideal co-captain
and will probably come in handy
when I routinely wander way ahead of my guys
to hang out with my dog and look at cool bugs."
And Jefferson is like "Yeah that sounds legit."

So Lewis and Clark get a crew together
called the CORPS OF DISCOVERY

and they buy all the necessary supplies
including a ton of beef jerky and bullets
plus a HUGE SACK OF BLUE BEADS
because I should probably explain
Lewis and Clark's mission has three parts:
1. Figure out how to get across America alive
2. Find as many cool bugs as possible
3. Make friends with all the natives
by giving them booze and shiny trash.
So they stock up on these beads
and by some crazy lucky coincidence
it turns out that for most of the native tribes
blue beads are like THE MOST SACRED BEADS.
They don't want no red beads
they don't want no black beads
they're sorta "eh" about white beads
but blue beads?
THOSE ARE THE SHIT.
Dudes will straight-up trade anything for blue beads
horses
meat
wives
whatever
and Lewis and Clark are like "Ha ha ha
we got these beads from China for like nothing.
Savages, am I right?"
DUDES
YOU THINK GOLD IS MONEY
GOLD:
THAT SHINY YELLOW METAL
THAT YOU FOUND IN A HILL
AND IS TOO SOFT TO MAKE ANYTHING
EXCEPT CERTAIN KINDS OF WIRE
WHICH YOU CAN'T EVEN MAKE
SO NOW WHO'S THE SAVAGES???

Anyway, these guys are not totally clueless
they hire some awesome translators and guides
like for example Sacagawea
who is married to this French fur trader
and seems to be the most stoic badass in the group
like, don't get me wrong
everyone is dealing with hardship
but only Sacagawea is dealing with that hardship
WHILE BIRTHING A GODDAMN CHILD
and then raising the child
(plus translating, plus guiding)
and being so chill about it
that Lewis is pretty sure she's actually a robot.
(Lewis is kind of a huge racist, by the way.)

Anyway they make it across the continent
they're all very pleased with themselves
but then
OH NO
THEY RUN OUT OF BLUE BEADS
THEY DIDN'T PACK ENOUGH BLUE BEADS
GREAT JOB, DICKBIRDS.
YOU WERE LAUGHING TO YOURSELVES
ABOUT HOW CHEAP THEY WERE
SO WHY DIDN'T YOU BUY MORE HUH?
Anyway, this puts them in a tough spot.
They have to eat their horses
and their shoes
they have to chop up their boats for firewood
they have to haul ass back home before they die
and the whole time
Lewis is just going fucking crazy
because he REALLY wants to get home
and also he was probably already crazy
so he keeps stealing shit from the natives
and almost throwing axes at them
and being like "Hey, gang

let's split up!
We'll cover more ground that way."

But in spite of Lewis's bullshit
all but one person makes it back home
and that one dude only doesn't make it
'cause he decided to keep hanging out in the woods
so that barely even counts
and Thomas Jefferson is like "Nice work.
Time to fill this land with white people!"
and Lewis is like "Okay, cool
glad you're satisfied
gonna go kill myself if that's okay."
and it's not okay at all, but it's too late, he's dead
and then Clark raises Sacagawea's kid for her
who grows up to be a badass mountain guide
and lives to be like eighty
and then dies on the way to get gold in Colorado
and by that time pretty much everyone else is dead
because that's how history works.

So basically
what I'm trying to say
is that your cross-country road trip game is weak.

★ ★ ★

Paul Bunyan Is Godzilla But with Thumbs

So now we've got all this land
but it's full of all these obnoxious trees.
Somebody's gotta do something about these trees.
NO PROBLEM, WE GOT LUMBERJACKS.
These are dudes
whose job is to MURDER ENTIRE FORESTS
IN STYLE
and one of the most prolific/preposterous tree-killers
is Paul "Biggie" Bunyan.

Now, I assume you've all heard of Paul Bunyan
you know
the single highest concentration of masculinity
ever to exist in one place at one time?
Oh yes
I'm talking about the dude who was SO BIG
that it took four storks to deliver him to his parents
SO BIG
that every time he cried
a swarm of frogs freaked out and fled the local pond
SO BIG
that when he outgrew his crib
his parents put him on a raft off the coast of Maine
because how do you feed a baby that big?

There are many stories about Paul
but since most of them are less stories
and more ridiculous short-form lies

how about instead of trying to reproduce one
I just walk you through a typical year in Paul's camp:

So you show up to this camp
and it's huge
like, gargantuan
like, way bigger than it needs to be.
They've used as much wood to make this camp
as they plan to cut down this whole goddamn year
and sitting in the middle of all this is Paul Bunyan
who is constantly smoking
(he smokes Peerless brand pipe tobacco, btw
because if there's one thing he's good at
it's being co-opted by advertisers)
and he blows all his smoke toward the West Coast
conveniently giving L.A. an excuse for all that smog.
It's hella wasteful
welcome to America.

As a logger in this camp, you are one of thousands
and all several thousand of you are lumberjacks
so of course you all need flapjacks
which means this camp is equipped with a griddle
SEVERAL MILES IN DIAMETER
which must be greased daily
by several dudes
with hog-skins strapped to their feet
SKATING ACROSS IT FROM END TO END.
I'M NOT MAKING THIS UP.
(SOMEONE ELSE MADE THIS UP.)

So once you've eaten your ridiculous breakfast
you head over to the woods to do some logging
but it's wintertime, and this is the worst winter ever
(every winter is the worst one ever in these stories).
The snow is deeper than the trees

also it's blue for some reason
also the ground is littered with FROZEN SNAKES
which you are expected to tie together
and use as sleds for the logs you cut down
which, may I remind you
ARE BURIED UNDER MILES OF BLUE SNOW.

But you do it anyway
because you're a tough-as-nails lumberjack
and also shit-scared of your enormous boss
and you get back to camp in the evening
to enjoy a hard-earned dinner
which is composed of pea soup
dispensed from an entire lake
which the cook made into pea soup
after accidentally dumping all the peas in there
plus you drink some Irish whiskey
made from potato skins
fermented by the withering gaze of Sour Pete
(who you are not looking forward to bunking with).
Then you go to sleep inside a hollow loaf of bread
along with all the other loggers
because that's how big the bread is here.
Everything is too big
it's like Texas, but also ridiculously cold.
It's only been one day, and you are already tired of it.

So through a combination of pancakes and fury
you make it through the winter of the blue snow
chop down an entire country's worth of trees
load them onto frozen snakes
and get them into the river
and you're riding the logs down the river
(this is an actual thing lumberjacks did)
when your logs get all out of whack
and run into each other, and get jammed
(this is the actual origin of the term "logjam").

So you're upset, obviously
but you're also looking forward to the time off
which is when Paul Bunyan shows up
with his giant ox
which is still pissed because the snow dyed
    it blue
and he puts the ox in the water
and just starts shooting it
over and over again
with a rifle.

And you're like "Dude what are you doing?"
and he's like "NO IT'S FINE
SHE JUST THINKS IT'S FLIES"
and sure enough, the ox starts swishing her tail
to get rid of the flies
and it makes the whole river flow backwards
unjamming your logs
and sending you on your way.

A few days later, you've finished your logging run
you're lounging with your bros at the camp
waiting for the season's pay
when Paul Bunyan comes thundering in
like "GUYS, GUYS
YOU KNOW THOSE TREES WE CUT DOWN?
THOSE WERE *GOVERNMENT TREES*
WE GOTTA GO, WE GOTTA GO NOW!"
So you freak out, obviously
(you are *not* going back to jail)
and you grab whatever's nearby
and book it for the nearest town.

Here's the thing though:
Paul Bunyan was lying to you
he just didn't have enough money to pay you guys.
Also, he's French-Canadian.

I don't know how you feel about that
but there it is.

The moral here is pretty obvious:
Folk heroes make terrible bosses.

★ ★ ★

THE BOOK OF MORMON:
GREAT MUSICAL,
BAD BOOK

Okay, so it's 600 BC
there's some Jews hanging out in Jerusalem
'cause where else are they gonna hang out, right?
Oh, wait
how about AMERICA?
Yeah see, this prophet Lehi has a vision
where God is like "DUDES
I MADE THIS GREAT PLACE
IT'S CALLED AMERICA
IT'S JUST SITTING OVER THERE
BETWEEN THE PACIFIC AND THE ATLANTIC
WOEFULLY UN-JEWED."
So Lehi and his bros get onto a boat
and sail to America
but when they get there, they notice a problem.
It is the same problem that Europeans will notice
when they show up about two thousand years later.
It is this:
America has abundant food and water
the deers and the antelopes are cavorting like hell
amber waves of grain all up ins
they've even got purple mountains
where do you find those, outside a hallucination?
AMERICA, THAT'S WHERE.
But there is one thing that America seems to lack:
BRUTAL WARS.

So the colonists are like "We better get on this."
They split up into two rival factions:
the Nephites and the Lamanites
I think the Nephites are the good guys
but I am too lazy to check.
It seems to me like they're all pretty sucky though
'cause how are you gonna try and fight a war
after you already traveled a million miles together?
That's like if I wanted to punch you in the face
and I was like "Hey, man
let's fly to Singapore"
and then when we got off the plane in Singapore
I punched you in the face.
. . . Okay, you know what
that would actually be hilarious.

Anyway they fight and fight
dudes die, it's awesome
but this whole time
the Nephites have been writing this shit down
in a book with golden pages.
I dunno how they found the time to get all that gold
seems like they're pretty busy fighting
but anyway they're writing and fighting
fighting and writing
in a language that no one else
in the history of anything
has ever heard of
called "reformed Egyptian"
which
from what I can tell
is made up mostly of sideways boobs
exclamation points
and different versions of the letter "T."

But then all of a sudden
JESUS APPEARS

YOU CANHAVE AS MANY
WIVES AS YOU WANT AS
LONG AS YOU WEAR WEIRD
UNDERWEAR AND NEVER
DRINK PEPSI

'cause he just got killed in Rome
and he is taking a vacation in America
before coming back to life.
He sees all these dudes fighting and he is like "WHOA
WHOA WHOA WHOA.
Didn't you guys get the memo?
No fighting!"
and then he has to explain everything to them
that he already explained to the other Jews
just to get them up to date
and I guess maybe he makes up some other stuff
about how you should have a ton of wives
and wear full-body underwear with holes in it
really solid advice
that he forgot to say the first time.

But all good things must come to an end.
Jesus goes to heaven
and everybody else dies
but not before making sure to bury their golden book

under a hill in upstate New York
you know, for posterity.

CUT TO 1832
some dude named Joe Smith is hanging out
in his house in upstate New York
when all of a sudden God is like "JOE
JOE!!!
THERE'S SOME GOLD PLATES IN THAT HILL.
I HAVE SUDDENLY CHOSEN YOU
TO GO DIG THEM UP.
GOOOOOOOO JOOOOOOOOOOOOOE."

So Joe goes over to the hill
and this angel appears like "'Ey buddy
I'm the angel Moroni."
(Moroni is one of the guys who wrote the book
the one with the with the gold plates
and also the last name of an Italian mob boss
played by Carl Weintraub on *Days of Our Lives*.
COINCIDENCE?)
So Joe is pretty impressed
but then the angel is like "Listen up, kiddo
I gots dese plates for youse
but you ain't gettin' nada
till you spend four years coming back hereabouts
and taking religion classes with yours truly
CAPISCE?"
And that is exactly what happens

So Joseph finally digs up these golden plates
but like I said
they're in "Reformed Egyptian"
so it's not like he can read them, right?
WRONG.
Clearly you have not heard of SEER STONES.
Here is how seer stones work:

Step 1: Take a rock
Step 2: Put the rock in a hat
Step 3: Put your face in the hat
Step 4: TRANSLATION COMPLETE
I am not exaggerating.
For several months Joseph Smith sits in his room
with his face inside a white stovepipe hat
shouting words at his scribe/investor Martin Harris.
Yes of course Joseph Smith needs investors
not like he could just sell pages
from that GOLDEN BOOK he found
that would be SACRILEGE.

So this goes on for a couple months
with only one false start
which only happens because Martin Harris's wife
(a confirmed FEMALE)
becomes suspicious of the fact
that no one except Joe has seen the gold book
which he apparently doesn't need to have with him
in order to translate
and which is written in a fake language
and is made out of gold
and says, amongst other things
that ancient Jews built boats and sailed to America
so she has the audacity to ask to see the translation
and finally does
and then STEALS it
which makes Joe SO MAD
that he decides not to re-translate the part she stole
and instead write a whole other part in two months
and then he has to get his buddy Harris
to take out some more loans to get the book printed
but that doesn't go so well
and Harris loses his house and his wife
which is okay because his wife sucked anyway.

ANYWAY
people are somewhat reluctant to believe in a book
that was written by staring into a hat full of rocks
but a lot of people are willing to make an exception
because it's the true word of God/they are bored
at which point the angel Moroni shows up again.
He's like "Hey, bub
I see you got a nice thing going here in New York
but, see, the trouble with New York
is that it's not nearly enough like ancient Jerusalem
by which I mean way underpopulated
and dry as a bullfrog's cooter.
Allow me to direct you
TO SALT LAKE CITY."
Except he's actually way more cagey than that
and Joseph dies on the way
without telling anybody exactly where they're going
and his buddy Brigham Young
(who has a name like an evangelical pedophile)
has to take over and lead them through the desert
until everyone gets sick of wandering around
and is just like "Fuck it
this is where we live now
let's wear white button-down shirts
and part our hair on the side
and ride bicycles forever and ever."
AND THAT'S WHERE MORMONS COME
    FROM.

So the moral of the story is
give a man a fish
and he'll eat for a day
give a man a hat full of rocks
and he'll move to a place where there are no fish.

★ ★ ★

THE TRAIL OF TEARS IS NOT THE NAME OF A LINKIN PARK ALBUM

So Indians . . .
YUP
THEY ARE STILL CALLED INDIANS
and they are still
(despite the best efforts of the colonists)
inhabiting a significant portion of their native lands.
This is a problem, and it must be stopped.
Luckily, President Andrew Jackson has this on lock.
This dude is a war hero
which the country just LOVES
and he is so good at war
that he has a nickname from it:
"Ol' Hickory"
meaning that he is strict I guess
(actually it sounds like a bondage thing to me).

Anyway, Andy slithers on into the White House
and immediately starts plotting to prank the natives.
He's like "Hey, [white] guys
remember all those promises we made to the Indians
about how they could keep their land and whatever?
How about
—and I'm just spitballin' here—
how about fuck those promises."
And pretty much everybody in Congress
most of whom stand to gain from this
is like "Hell yeah, kick 'em out!"

This screws over a whole lot of tribes
but for the sake of time
let's focus on a prime example:
the Cherokee Nation.

The Cherokees have busted their asses for YEARS
to make white people like them
they have taken up farming
slave-owning
speaking English
wearing stupid bow ties
all the hallmarks of true civilization
and they rightly expect that as a result of this
they will be treated by the Europeans
the same way the Europeans treat each other.
The problem here
is that the Cherokees do not know European history.

All this assimilation means
that when the order comes down to vacate
the Cherokees are in a prime position to argue.
They know the law
plus they have their own politicians.
One of them is named John Ross
he's the son of a Scotsman and a Cherokee
which makes him automatically respectable.
The other guy is named John Ridge
and is closer to full-blooded Cherokee
but he went to college and his name is John
so that at least counts for something.

So pretty early on, John Ross gets elected chief
and the first thing he does
is he draws up a constitution
and does everything he can to be like "Hey
the Cherokee Nation

IS ACTUALLY A FUCKING NATION"
but Andrew Jackson is still like "Naw"
so John Ross TAKES HIS ASS TO COURT.

And he wins!
The Supreme Court is like "Actually, Mr. President
it turns out you can't just issue a proclamation
declaring that other people's land is now yours
it turns out that that's called stealing."
So the Cherokees are like "Ha HA!"
And Andrew Jackson is like "Well
if the Supreme Court hates stealing so much
let them enforce that law."
BECAUSE YEAH, ANDREW JACKSON
THAT'S *SO* WHAT THE JUDICIARY IS FOR.
Then he turns around and tells Georgia
(which really wants the Cherokees' land)
to just go nuts and start killing whoever.
THIS DUDE GETS TO BE ON THE TWENTY
ALEXANDER HAMILTON IS ON THE TEN
AND HE INVENTED THE NATIONAL BANK.
WHAT
THE
HELL.

But John Ross (and most of his tribe)
are still like "Hell no, we won't go"
which is upsetting to John Ridge
because John Ridge's dad is pretty rich
from owning slaves and a cotton plantation
and doesn't want to get into a fight with the U.S.
So Ridge tries to get elected chief
but John Ross is just like "WHOOPS
looks like I accidentally suspended elections
it's an emergency, bitch, step the fuck back."
So John Ridge is like "Okay, fine"

GIVE A WHITE MAN AN INCH & HE WILL TAKE EVERYTHING YOU LOVE

and then he just goes to the U.S. government himself
and signs a treaty
that he has NO AUTHORITY TO SIGN
giving up the rights to all that tasty land.

So all the Cherokees are like "WTF, JOHN?"
and John Ross is like "Don't worry, guys
I may have the same first name as that douche
but I am going to fix this."
So he goes the way of the impotent Internet denizen
and starts a petition
he gets fifteen thousand signatures
which accomplishes jack shit
because on the day congress is supposed to read it
two senators get into a duel
and one dies
and government is canceled for a week.
This . . .
this is civilization.

A few months later, Georgia is like "TIME'S UP"
and they show up with a big ol' army
drag everyone out of their houses
and force march them eight hundred and fifty
    miles
in the dead of winter
with basically no preparation
to a shittier spot across the Mississippi
which they will kick them out of forty years later.

Naturally, a whole bunch of people die
and the rest of them are irreparably scarred
but luckily John Ross manages to cheer them up
by actually establishing a government for a bit
and that goes super duper well
until after the Civil War

when the Americans are done killing each other
and decide they need someone else to fuck with.

So the moral of the story
is never get between a white man
and an ocean.

★ ★ ★

I Am Too Drunk to Remember the Alamo

Okay, so the Alamo happens
and a bunch of famous dudes die, the end.

Oh, what, you want more details?
Are you trying to tell me
YOU DON'T REMEMBER THE ALAMO???
Wow, guys
I knew when I was writing this book
that I would have to educate y'all a LITTLE
but your ignorance is staggering me right now.
Okay, fine, let's do this.

So Mexico owns Texas
and Texas is full of Americans
but it's okay
because up to this point, Mexico has been pretty chill
what with having a federal government and all
but then Mexico's like "Wait a second . . .
you know what's better than a federal government?
A TOTALITARIAN DICTATORSHIP.
WOOOOO."
And Texas is like "Oh no you di-int."

To be fair, Texas isn't alone in this.
Most people in Mexico are pretty pissed
and a lot of them fight wars about it
but of all the provinces that rebel against Mexico
Texas is by far the loudest about it
and has continued to be the loudest about it

all the way to the present day
so we're going to focus on Texas in this story
because if there's one thing history is short on
it's stories about white dudes shooting things.

So Texas has an army
and Mexican dictator/general Santa Anna isn't pleased
so he gets himself a bigger army
and stomps into Texas to kill everybody.
He is headed straight for this town called Bexar
which is guarded by this fort called the Alamo
which used to be a mission
and a hospital
but is now just a place to shoot guns out of.

Now, there's a guy at the Alamo
named William Travis
and he doesn't wanna die
so he starts calling up any dude he can find
who might possibly be the general of the Texan army
(fun fact:
most kinds of mud
are better organized than the Texan army at this time)
and he's like "Could you help a brother out?"
and finally he gets in touch with Sam Houston
who he should have tried first
since he has a city in Texas named after him
and Sam is like "Nah, I think you're screwed.
Actually I'm just gonna send one of my guys
to take all your cannons so the Mexicans can't."
And Travis is like "Whoa, harsh."

But Houston makes a critical mistake:
as his cannon-taking emissary
he selects none other
than Jim "I got a knife named after me" Bowie
possibly the least responsible person in the West.

Bowie shows up at the Alamo
sees that the odds are impossible
and goes "Yup.
Looks like I'm staying here
along with the soldiers Sam sent with me.
Hope you guys like dying, because that's the plan."
So the soldiers at the fort elect him commander
OBVIOUSLY
and Bowie is like "WOOOO!"
and goes into town and gets shitfaced
and then comes back in the morning
like "It's okay, Travis
you can be co-commander."
and the whole time Travis is like "What."

Then more dudes show up
the most important being Davy Crockett
the former U.S. senator/bear-puncher
who famously claimed he could
"swallow a Mexican whole without choking
if you butter his head and pin his ears back."
Which is either a threat or a sex thing or both.
Either way
Travis quickly realizes shit is getting out of hand
so he keeps sending out notes like "Please, anyone
I am going to die in a church full of psychopaths
send food or something, come on."

But all of a sudden Santa Anna is here
and he has made a new rule
which is that all Texan rebels now count as pirates.
He does this to allow himself to auto-execute them
instead of taking prisoners
but the actual effect of this declaration
is to make it so that instead of fighting just cowboys
he is now fighting COWBOY PIRATES.
This is a DANGEROUS MOVE.

Santa Anna hangs out by the Alamo for two weeks
firing cannonballs into the fort
which the defenders scoop up and fire back at him
until finally he's like "Screw this" and just attacks.
He has way more guys than the Texans do
like, ten to one
plus the Texans are mostly out of ammo and food.
So what do they do?
Do they run away like intelligent humans?
NO.
They stand their ground
and club their enemies with their empty rifles
like HEROES.

Even Jim Bowie
who is sick in bed
(probably from drinking too hard)
manages to get in on the action
by just waiting in his room
and shooting or stabbing every fool who busts in
until he runs out of bullets/knife
and they kill him with bayonets.
I feel like Bowie's death is a rare example
of someone who died sick in bed
of multiple fresh stab wounds.

Anyway, yeah, all the Texans die.
What did you think was gonna happen?
I mean, they kill a lot of Mexicans
so that's cool, I guess
as cool as killing a lot of people can ever be
and the Mexicans end up so confused and angry
that they keep firing at the dead bodies
and at each other, sometimes
for like fifteen minutes
until Santa Anna finally has to be like "Uh, hey
we won!

Retreat, guys!
Those dead bodies aren't getting up!"
Then he executes all his prisoners.

So what was the point of all this?
The Alamo got sacked
and Santa Anna kept marching
but
and this is crucial
he came out of it looking like a total dick
for murdering all those starving outnumbered Texans
and killing the prisoners
and I'm sure he felt sort of bad about himself
at least for a little while.

This highlights the true importance of the Alamo
as possibly the first recorded instance
of aggressive passive aggression.

★ ★ ★

Bre'r Rabbit Is the Bugs Bunny of Folk Heroes

So one thing that happens
when you get kidnapped from your homeland
and forced to work for free in a foreign country
is that you tend to bring your stories with you
because you need something to entertain you
while you hate your life.
The other thing that happens, though
is that your stories start to get seriously mixed up
with all the stories in the foreign country you're in
so for example
all over Africa, back in the day
ladies and dudes were telling stories about tricksters.
Some of these tricksters were spiders
some were rabbits
but all of them were HUGE assholes
and when these huge imaginary assholes
found their way to the land of opportunity
they got mashed together with some Cherokee tales
and some down-home country agriculture
and suddenly they were all about a dude
named Bre'r Rabbit.

Now, Bre'r Rabbit
(Brer Rabbit for short)
is the quintessential motherfucker
he likes to swagger around
stealing shit and laughing about it.
And Bre'r Fox
(Brer Fox for short)
is essentially the Wile E. Coyote

to Brer Rabbit's Road Runner
and together
these two wacky animals
have a wild and wonderful history
of getting co-opted by white writers
who then make a ton of money off of them.
So, uh . . . allow me.

One day Brer Fox wakes up like
"Damn, I really wanna kill Brer Rabbit
before he steals any more of my stuff.
Oh man, I have the ultimate plan:
I'm gonna make a baby
OUT OF TAR."

So Brer Fox buys some tar from ACME
and mixes it up real good
and then makes a baby out of it
and puts a big wide-brimmed hat on the baby
you know
like babies tend to wear
and he places it right in the center of the road.
The myth says that this was like the cutest baby ever
but I don't know how cute a baby can be
when it is made out of DEADLY TAR.

ANYWAY
Brer Fox goes over and hides in the bushes
so excited about his incredibly stupid plan
and Brer Rabbit comes whistling along
and he sees this baby
and he is like "Whoa
what is this fine baby doing in the road?
Hey, baby, how you doin'?"
and the baby is like
" . . ."
so then Brer Rabbit gets kind of mad

because he likes it when people talk to him
so he can mock whatever they're saying
and he is like "Now, baby
if you do not immediately start talking to me
I AM GOING TO PUNCH YOU IN THE FACE."
Not even stopping to consider that maybe
JUST MAYBE
the tar baby is too young to talk
or you know
that it is MADE OF TAR
No, he just shouts at that inanimate baby
until finally he gets so mad
he really does smack it upside the head
and what do you think happens?
HIS PAW GETS STUCK.

So what do you think he does?
he says, "BABY
MAKE YOUR FACE LET GO OF MY PAW
OR I WILL SMACK YOUR FACE AGAIN
WITH MY OTHER PAW."
And the baby does no such thing
so true to his word
Brer Rabbit hits the baby again
and his OTHER paw gets stuck
and he is like "RRR I'M SO MAD
MAYBE KICKING YOU WILL HELP???"
but it predictably does not
in fact it just makes things much much worse
so then I guess Brer Rabbit is just like "Welp
I've already fucked up almost as hard as possible.
Might as well hit this baby with my face too."
so he does
and it is in this undignified state
that Brer Fox finds him:
covered in tar with his fists inside a baby.

So Brer Fox is of course extremely pleased by this
and is like "Ohhhhh Brer Rabbit
I have wanted to kill you for SOOOOO LONG.
I don't even want to eat you
just kill you.
Hmm . . . how should I kill you, Brer Rabbit?
Should I roast you?
Nah, too much effort.
Maybe I should set you on fire?
No, too similar to roasting.
What do you think, Brer Rabbit?
How should I kill you?"

And Brer Rabbit thinks fast
and he says
"PLEASE BRER FOX
ROAST ME
FLAMBEE ME
I DON'T CARE
JUST WHATEVER YOU DO
PLEEEEEEEASE
DON'T THROW ME INTO THAT BRIAR PATCH
THE ONE RIGHT OVER THERE."

Now if I was gonna kill a rabbit
and a rabbit said that to me
first of all I'd be like holy shit a talking rabbit
and maybe question my sanity a little
but after we'd sorted everything out
I'd probably just say okay
and throw him in a fire
because I am a merciful person
who still really likes killing rabbits.
But Brer Fox has the rare talent
of being exactly as stupid as he is lazy
so he is like "Hm

that briar patch does appeal to both my sadism
AND my laziness.
It'll tear you to pieces.
I'MA THROW YOU IN THE BRIAR PATCH."
And Brer Rabbit is like "NO NO NO NO
ANYTHING BUT THAT"
and Brer Fox is like "FAT CHUCKLES, GRANDMA
IN YOU GO."
and chucks him in.

But as he's lying in the middle of the road
giggling to himself
he suddenly realizes
he is not the only one giggling
so he looks up
and at the top of a nearby hill
there's Brer Rabbit
laughing and combing tar out of his hair
and he is like "You perfect idiot
I was born and bred in a briar patch
BORN AND FUCKING BRED
DO YOU UNDERSTAND???"
And Brer Fox is like "No, I do not understand.
Like, I get that you were born inside a horrible plant
but I don't see how that magically cleaned off the tar
or what it has to do with anything, really."
But Brer Rabbit doesn't hear him
Because he's too busy stealing stuff
and punching real babies to make up for lost time.

And that, friends
is how Brer Rabbit invented reverse psychology
which just goes to show
that you can be as stupid as you want
as long as your enemies are a lot stupider.

★ ★ ★

Harriet Tubman Has
Seizures for Justice

Harriet Tubman was literally Moses
that's what she was actually called
by the slaves
that she led out of Egypt
I mean the South.
She was a hard-walking
tough-talking
constantly hallucinating
secret agent OF JUSTICE
but before I tell you all about Harriet T
let's talk a little about her worst enemy:
SLAVERY.

See, many centuries in the past
a bunch of dudes discovered this sweet life hack
where you could force people to work for free.
They called this life hack "slavery"
and it took the world many years to patch it
(the patch is still not available in some places).
Some countries took especially long to do this
like for example AMERICA
LAND OF THE FREE.
Like, Benjamin Franklin freed his slaves
and G. Washington freed (some of) his slaves
and Thomas Jefferson said slaves should be free
while simultaneously banging one of his slaves
but the U.S. Constitution back in the day
had a critical glitch that made changing things hard.
It was called the three-fifths compromise
and here is how it worked:

Basically, when the constitution got written
the South wanted their slaves to count as population
so that they could have more representatives
and the North was like "But guys, slaves can't vote
meaning they can't select representatives
so that's not exactly fair.
How about we say slaves are worth . . . I dunno
three-fifths of a person each?"
and the South is like "NOW WHO'S THE RACIST?"
but it still means the South gets repped way harder
which means anytime anyone tries to end slavery
the slave-owning states are just like "NOPE."

So for slaves at this time
waiting for slavery to be outlawed is not a good plan
there is only one good plan
and it is disguised as a terrible plan:
RUN AWAY.

No one has a better excuse to run away
than young Harriet "Minty" Tubman.
Her daily routine is basically "wake up
get assigned random household task
be too inexperienced to do assigned task
get beaten until too weak to do assigned task
get beaten
do task somehow
. . . sleep?"
One day, one of her fellow slaves tries to run
and their master responds in the only sane way
which is to throw a lead weight at HER head
which does not stop the other guy from escaping
but DOES give Harriet epilepsy
so . . . win-win?

Now at this point
Minty's already tried to escape once

and a projectile to the brain is a great motivator
so when she finds out she's gonna be sold to Georgia
which is basically the Silicon Valley of slavery
she escapes!
Via the Underground Railroad!

WHAT IS THE UNDERGROUND RAILROAD?
WHO THE FUCK KNOWS??
The problem with a covert network of safe houses
illegally smuggling slaves to freedom
is that if you are part of this network
you are not gonna wanna keep a ton of records
and all the slaves who escape via this network
are super careful about not dropping any spoilers
seeing as they have family and friends down south
who they presumably would like to see freed.
All we really know about it
is that folks hid slaves in their houses during
    the day
(the houses were called "stations")
other folks led them at night
(these people were called "conductors")
other folks just donated money
(these dudes were called "investors")
and everyone involved really liked train metaphors
(they were what are known as "railfans").

So Harriet escapes via this network
leaving behind her parents
her brothers and sisters
and her husband
who is actually not even a slave
so who the hell knows why he doesn't go
    with her.
Probably he's afraid of commitment.
Oh well
his loss.

After such a miraculous escape
a normal person would have just chilled out
but Harriet Tubman is not a normal person
she is an escaped slave with a brain injury
so she immediately embarks on a new mission
entitled "OPERATION: FREE EVERY SLAVE
ESPECIALLY MY FAMILY."
She does this for TEN YEARS
and during that time she never fucks up once
assisted as she is by her CRAZY-PERSON VISION.
Seriously, she has seizures that predict danger
it's awesome, you should listen to your seizures.

This whole mission of hers is made more difficult
by the fact that immediately after she escapes
the government not only fails to end slavery
but passes a NEW SHITTY LAW
called the Fugitive Slave Act
which says "Hey
you know how slavery is illegal in the North?
Well, you can still catch escaped slaves up there
in fact, how about this:
You can just grab any black dude you want
tell a judge he's an escaped slave
and we will PAY THE JUDGE to agree with you."
And all the slave states are like "HELL YEAH"
and all the slaves are like "HELL NO"
so slaves don't just have to get out of the South
they have to get to CANADA.
Yes, Canada
"like America, but without all that shit you hate."

But Harriet don't care
she's leading dudes through swamps
pretending to buy dudes at auctions
then stealing them instead
hiding in rivers to avoid dogs

planning armed slave rebellions
just flipping off the whole entire concept of slavery
until her hands are just two giant middle fingers.
It is inconvenient for using chopsticks
but excellent for making a point.

Then the Civil War happens
and Harriet is like "Shit yeah, let's end slavery."
So she signs up as a nurse
and treats black dudes FOR FREE
and when they start letting black people fight
she dresses up in the most legit battle dress ever
and leads an armed raid
that frees about 750 slaves
and then she raises her staff and frogs rain from the sky
covering the entire South in a mass of ribbiting flesh.
I may have made part of that up.

After the war ends, Harriet goes back to Canada
and on the train, the conductor is like
"Hey, why are you sitting in the soldiers' section?
One, you are a woman
two, you are black
three, I am a terrible person."
And Harriet is like "Okay
one, I'm the first woman to lead an armed Union raid
two, fuck you
three, I'm a conductor on the Underground Railroad
so maybe YOU should give me YOUR seat
bitch."
The conductor does not take kindly to this
so he throws her off the train
thus beginning a proud American tradition
of throwing important black people off public transit.

After that, Harriet lives for a stupidly long time
making money by letting people write her biography
which is a pretty baller way to make money
but she's still way poor
because the army won't pay her any pension
you know, because racism
but at least slavery is over
right?

. . . Right?
Well, anyway
What we can learn from Harriet Tubman
is that sometimes the most badass thing you can do
is run away from your problems.

★ ★ ★

Abraham Lincoln Is as Tall as He Is Tall

POPULAR MISCONCEPTION:
Abe Lincoln was born in a log cabin
WHICH HE BUILT HIMSELF.
Fact:
He may or may not have been born in a log cabin
and he definitely built a log cabin later
when he was working for his farmer dad
but regardless, there is a type of log named after him
which is used for building tiny cabins
and that's what matters.
That, and he's ridiculously tall.

But Lincoln stops being a farm guy pretty fast
gets hella popular
and picks up the nickname "Honest Abe"
without chopping down any cherry trees or anything
which is why when he runs for Congress, he wins
(eventually)
and then while he is in Congress
one of his buddies is like "Dude
you know what you'd be great at?
LAWYERING"
so that's what Abe does for many years.
He makes fat stacks with the lawyer gig
(fat stacks being a prerequisite for real politics)
and he's also a super nice dude
so it's only a matter of time
before he gets to be president.

Here's the problem, though:
Abe is a Republican
and he really hates slavery.
Now, these things are not a problem by themselves
but there are a bunch of dudes
(mostly the Democrats, but also some Republicans)
who really LIKE slavery
primarily because they are not themselves slaves.
Even THIS would not be a problem normally
except that the U.S. has just bought a ton of land
(from Napoleon, because he's strapped for cash)
and Lincoln doesn't want any slavery in the new land
so he's trying to convince all these super racist bros
to do this thing he wants
and the way he does it
is by trying REALLY HARD
to sound *just racist enough*
all like "Guys, I don't like black people THAT much
I mean I still TOTALLY think they're subhuman
I just don't think forced labor is okay maybe?"
and even that weak-sauce stance
is not enough to placate the crazy racists.

So when Lincoln runs for president, it's a shit show.
He's got a Democrat running against him
and a pro-slavery Republican
which has the unexpected effect
of splitting the pro-slavery votes
plus a bunch of states don't even bother to vote
because they can't stand to be part of a country
that even allows an anti-slavery guy to RUN
which means they aren't voting against him
so suddenly Lincoln is president
with like 40 percent of the vote
which means about 40 percent of people are happy.
Shit like this never ends well.

So as soon as Lincoln gets inaugurated
like half the United States ragequits the Union
and they form their own club, called the Confederacy
and Lincoln is like "Guys, chill out
you can totally keep your slaves
beat the shit out of them, I don't care
I just don't want any NEW slave states
and I think you should stay part of my country
and also I think you're all terrible people."

Naturally the Confederacy is havin' none of this.
They elect their own president
and raise an army
and take over all the federal property in their states.
Example:
Virginia has surrounded this one fort, called Sumter
which still belongs to the Union.
The dudes inside of it are getting super hungry
also nervous
but no one is firing their guns
because nobody wants to be the one to start a war
so finally, Lincoln is like "Okay, guys
just gonna send some food to my bros at the fort
no guns or anything
definitely not a military action.
Boy it sure would suck if you shot this caravan
then I'd have no choice but to declare war."
GUESS WHAT:
GUNFIRE.

For the next four years, war is all Lincoln does
he checks out war books from the library
he writes angry letters to all his generals
and ends up firing like half of them
until he finally lands on Ulysses S. Grant.
Meanwhile, all these abolitionists and escaped slaves

are like "Hey, Lincoln
remember how you hate slavery?
Thinking about ending it anytime soon, buddy?"
and Lincoln is like "GIVE ME A BREAK, GUYS
some of our allies have slaves
and I reeeeeeally don't want to upset them right now
so maybe we hold off a little?"
and everyone is like "But Lincoln
if we free the slaves, we can get them to fight for us"
and Lincoln is like "SOLD."

So he writes a letter to the Confederacy
like "Dear jerks,
All your slaves are free now.
Have fun with that.
Love, Abe."
And the Confederacy is like "You can't do that!"
but all their slaves are like "HE TOTALLY CAN."
So now all these slaves are running away
and Lincoln is like "Oh shit
might have to start treating these people like humans
can we get some constitutional amendments up ins?
BOOM, 13th Amendment: Slavery is over
14th Amendment: Everybody is citizens
15th Amendment: Black dudes can vote
not women though
that would be CRAZY.
All right, I gotta go win this war.
You're welcome."

So the war ends
and Abe gets to officially say slavery is over
but then he makes the literally fatal mistake
of going to a theater to celebrate
and some dick named John runs in and shoots him
simultaneously ending his life
and freeing him up for a career as a vampire hunter.

So
he has a big funeral
and ex-slave / star abolitionist Fred Douglass comes
and Douglass is like "Good job, Abe Lincoln
still pretty sure you were a racist though.
Rest in peace, dude."
Later they make a statue of him
that makes him look like Zeus.
It's inappropriate
because everyone knows
that Abraham Lincoln
is actually America's JESUS.

So the moral of the story
is you should never go see plays
live theater is dead.

★ ★ ★

Sarah Emma Edmonds Might Actually Be Your Dad and You Would Never Know

Unlike the Revolutionary War
which was fought because a group of rich white guys
(who happened to own slaves)
didn't like the dude in charge of their country
and decided to start a new one
(SO NOBLE!)
the CIVIL war
is fought because some slave-owning white guys
(who happen to be rich)
don't like the dude in charge of their country
and decide to start a new one.
(SO TERRIBLE!)
Dudes on both sides of the Mason-Dixon Line
(the imaginary line that marks where slavery is)
are joining up left and right
to fight for this hella just cause.
This cause is so hella just that even LADIES want in
but the Union Army is like a vast treehouse
with "NO GIRLS ALLOWED" scrawled on the front
which stops most ladies from getting in on the fun.
Sarah Emma Edmonds is not most ladies.

Emma can't legally join the army because vagina
but here's the thing:
She REALLY wants to
so what does she do?

She mans up
LITERALLY
by dressing as a dude named Franklin Thomas
and then bluffs her way past the recruiters
whose rigorous medical screening process
basically just consists of making sure she has hands.

So now she's in the army
working as a nurse, 'cause that's what she wanted
but anyone who is willing to cross-dress for freedom
is not gonna be satisfied nursing for very long.
When an old homie of hers gets shot while scouting
and another Union dude gets shot for spying
she's like hm . . .
I'm already basically spying in this army
might as well become a DOUBLE-SPY

So she goes to her boss, General McClellan
who has NO IDEA she's a lady
and she's like "Hey, I hear you need spies"
and he's like "Do you love freedom?"
and she's like "Shit yeah"
and he's like "Do you know military stuff?"
and she's like "Yup I read some books"
and he's like "Let me feel the bumps on your skull"
and she's like ". . . What?"
and he's like "Don't diss phrenology, it's totally real"
and she's like ". . . What?"
and he's like "The bumps tell me you're hired
you start in three days
not gonna train you at all
figure it out"
and Emma's like ". . . Okay, sure."

So she's like "Hm, I need a disguise.
Guess I could just go as a woman.
That's lame though.

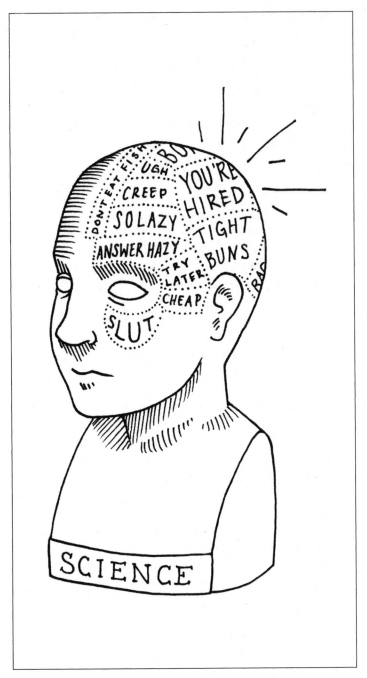

How about I go as a BLACK MAN.
YES, EXCELLENT."
So she buys a woolly wig from a minstrel show
(hooray for racism)
dyes her skin black with silver nitrate
names herself "Cuff"
and then shows up in Yorktown
behind Confederate lines
like "'Sup, guys, I'm a slave and I'm lost
plz show me all your military defenses."
AND IT WORKS.

So when a dumb Rebel officer puts her on guard duty
she escapes back to the Union side
and she gets to keep the gun he gave her as a prize
and go back to working as a nurse
FOR LIKE TEN MINUTES
before McClellan is like "Hey, Frank
(I still don't suspect that you are a lady)
we need some more facts about enemies.
Can you hook us up?"

This time Emma decides to take it easy
and go dressed as a lady
OH, NOPE, TOO EASY
make that a fifty-year-old Irish lady
named Bridget O'Shea.
So she sneaks into Rebel territory on a boat
and accidentally finds a dying dude in an old house
who she takes care of until he dies
and he gives her a gold watch
to deliver to a major in the Confederate camp
and she's like "Oh no, so sad, he died"
but she's also like "YESSSS ULTIMATE COVER."

I should mention at this point
that when Emma goes a-spying

she NEVER HAS AN ESCAPE PLAN
she just shows up in a fancy costume
and expects that some chumpalicious soldier
will at some point bend over backwards
to make sure she can leave with all their secrets.
THIS IS ALWAYS WHAT HAPPENS.

Like, she shows up to the camp
makes friends with the major
sells everybody soap
learns all about their defenses
and then they GIVE HER A HORSE
and ask her to lead them to the dead dude's body
which she does
shortly before disappearing on her new horse
which she names "Rebel," just to rub it in.

She keeps pulling this shit for a while
delivering top-secret messages
and exploiting slavery for covert data.
At one point she moves to Kentucky
poses as a young Canadian gentleman
and becomes the accountant
for the HEAD OF A REBEL SPY
    RING
who she then totally ruins.

And this WHOLE TIME
nobody in the Union figures out that she's a chick
She is a double agent in the best possible way
until she comes down with malaria
and she's like "Aw shoot
if I go to the hospital tent to get fixed
they will take off my clothes and see my boobs
that will be totally embarrassing/ruin my career
OH WELL, GUESS I BETTER DESERT."
So she runs away to DC

changes back into a girl
and works as a nurse for the rest of the war.

After the war is over
she calls up her old war buddies
and she's like "Hey
remember that dude Frank Thompson?
Yeah, that was me."
And they're like "WHAT?!"
And she's like "Yeah. So hey, I need a favor
could you come tell Congress that I'm me?
I wanna get a military pension
also an honorable discharge."
And they're like "Sure, no problem."
So that happens
and Emma eventually gets married and has kids
and lives a pretty boring life
because she used up all her adrenaline in the army.

So the moral of the story
is that if you assume every man you meet
is a woman in disguise
it will make bus rides way more entertaining.

JOHN HENRY WORKS
HIMSELF TO DEATH

So after the Civil War
slavery is officially over
yayyyyy!
But there are still a lot of dudes
who got super used to owning slaves
so even though they can't own slaves
they figure out that they can still give ex-slaves jobs
that are a whole lot LIKE slavery.
Let's take fictional man-drill John Henry, for example.

Now, John Henry was a steel-drivin' man.
I SAID
JOHN HENRY WAS A STEEL-DRIVIN' MAN.

Do you guys know what that means?
That means that he was a dude
whose job
was to KILL MOUNTAINS.

Now, the way he did this
was that some poor son of a bitch named Little Bill
would hold a steel drill in place against the rock
while John Henry BEAT ON IT
AS HARD AS HE COULD
WITH A TWENTY-POUND HAMMER
and Bill had to turn the drill after every strike
and eventually the drill would get dull
so he had to swap it out
for another drill
that someone would hopefully hand to him

WITHOUT MISSING A BEAT
and then they would take the old drill to a blacksmith
so the blacksmith could fix it
and then bring it back to Bill
so he could switch it out AGAIN
and meanwhile
John Henry's hammer is whistling past Bill's junk
or face, or ribs, or wherever he has to hold the drill
in order to brutalize the rock in the right direction.

Meanwhile, John Henry has it easy.
All HE has to do
is heft a TWENTY-POUND HAMMER
over and over again
with perfect accuracy
all day
burrowing through solid rock
never stopping, never getting tired
under constant threat of massive rock slides.

So this is this guy's job.

Now, John Henry works for a pack of rat bastards
called the C&O Railroad Company.
One day John Henry's railroad team arrives
at this BIG, BIG MOUNTAIN
and the railroad crew is all like "Oh wow, bummer.
Guess we better start going around this mountain."
And aforementioned rat bastards from C&O
are like "NOPE.
GOIN' STRAIGHT THROUGH.
IT IS ONLY LIKE A MILE AND A HALF THICK.
YOU GUYS LIKE HAVING JOBS, RIGHT?
SO *DO IT*."

So they do it.
Most of these guys are freed slaves

so they don't exactly have their pick of employment.
This goes double for John Henry
who, like Nicki Minaj's ass
DOES NOT QUIT.
(Note:
This is basically the only trait John Henry shares
with Nicki Minaj's ass.)
So every day all the steel-drivers go to work
and they fling themselves at this mountain
and like twenty people die
but John Henry just keeps abusing that stone
making a solid ten-foot tunnel every day, at LEAST.
So, you know, great for him
but all his friends are still dead
and the dicks at C&O are getting impatient
so when this traveling salesman shows up
with a steam-powered drill machine
they are like "SIGN US UP.
P.S.: Everyone who works for us is fired now.
ESPECIALLY JOHN HENRY."

Now, John Henry takes guff from no man.
It is unreal how little guff this guy takes.
Like, if there were a great big pile of guff
just laying by the side of the road
and John Henry walked by
that pile would remain completely undisturbed
because he would take none of it.
So when he sees this guff coming his way
he just sidesteps the lot of it
and then he turns around like "Hey
traveling salesman
I bet I can drill harder, better, faster, AND stronger
than your candy-assed machine."
And the traveling salesman is like "YOU'RE ON."
So John Henry lines up next to this machine
along with his trusty shaker Little Bill

and TWO TWENTY-POUND HAMMERS
and they get
to
work.

So John and the drill are staying pretty much tied
maybe the drill is even doing a little better
but then it gets STUCK in a hole in the rock
and John Henry just goes grunting and flailing away
FOURTEEN FEET INTO THAT MOUNTAIN.
BAM CLINK CACHANG POW BOOM PEW PEW
I DON'T KNOW HOW A HAMMER SOUNDS.

So, final score:
Newfangled steam drill: nine feet.
One man armed only with sweat and hammers:
fourteen feet.
Oh wait.
John Henry was using two hammers
so he drilled TWO HOLES
so really, the score was nine to TWENTY-EIGHT.
Yeah.

But there's some bad news too.
As soon as he finds out his score
John Henry puts down his hammers and dies
because he just hammered that rock so hard
he gave himself a stroke.
It doesn't say in the ballad
but I like to think that his last words
were something like
". . . Damn right."

Anyway, then he's dead
so they end up using the steam drill anyway
although they have to cancel work for like a week
because everyone thinks John's ghost is in the tunnel

also the tunnel turns out to be way unstable
because it is a bad idea to use contests
to construct delicate railway tunnels.

But none of that matters
because the real hero of this story
is Little Bill
who held two drills
right next to all the tenderest parts of his body
against a solid stone wall
while a muscular dude repeatedly charged at him
flailing two twenty-pound hammers.
And he kept holding those drills
and turning them
and shaking out the stone debris
and switching out the drills when they got dull
FOR THIRTY-FIVE MINUTES
AND TWENTY-EIGHT FEET
and he *didn't* have a stroke
or even poop himself a little.

So let's hear it for Little Bill
the real American hero.

★ ★ ★

CUSTER'S LAST STAND IS HIGHLY UNNECESSARY

So the Union wins the Civil War
(spoilers)
and slavery is over(?)
but there is still a problem
America is just CRAWLING with Indians
and all the REAL Americans
(that is
the white dudes who showed up a few years ago)
are like "We've been in this country for a while now
it is pretty clear to us that this is not India
so obviously these Indians do not belong here
let's murder them until they leave."

Except, it's a little more complicated than that.
Sure, some dudes just wanna kill Indians
but for some dudes
(and these dudes are considered *Indian sympathizers*)
it's just like when a cat is sitting in your chair
and you're like "Okay, cat
I'm going to sit down in this chair now
and if you are under my butt when that happens
well, that's on you
literally."
Except instead of a chair it is all of North America
and instead of a butt it's millions of white people
and instead of getting sat on
it is total annihilation.
So on the one side you have gung-ho murderers
and on the other side
you have people who just don't give a shit.

Luckily, the U.S. hits upon a brilliant strategy
this strategy is to make treaties with Indian
    chiefs
(none of whom have the authority to do this
because being an Indian chief
is sort of like being Benedict Cumberbatch:
Everybody likes you
but nobody has to do what you say)
and then, once they make these treaties
they break the treaties
pretty much immediately
and if any Indians complain about it
they shoot them and their entire families
and then set their whole village on fire.
It's a pretty killer strategy.

Obviously this pisses some Indians off
specifically a big group known as the Sioux
which is a French word for "enemies"
and therefore pretty biased
so I'm going to call them what they call themselves:
Lakota
which basically means "friends."
This is also pretty biased
but way easier to type than Sioux.

When I say the Lakota are pissed off
I mean SOME of the Lakota are pissed off
other Lakota just want to make peace.
But all the peace guys get massacred
because they're way easier for white dudes to find
being as they are hanging out near white settlements
TRYING TO MAKE PEACE.
So pretty soon, all the Lakota
(and most of the Cheyenne
who have been having the same problems)
are ready to rumble.

But when I say "ready to rumble"
I mean "ready to be attacked."
Like, they don't go running all over the place
setting random houses on fire.
They mostly stay home
inside the bounds of the latest bullshit treaty
and occasionally blow up a railroad agent
or show up to a treaty negotiation
just to tell the U.S. delegation how full of shit it is.
Obviously, they must be stopped.

THANK GOD FOR GEORGE CUSTER.
George (whose middle name is ARMSTRONG)
is an arrogant, violent, bigoted maniac
who dresses like he's cosplaying as a cowboy
at a time when there are STILL REAL COWBOYS
mostly because he is in love with these novels
written by a guy named James Fenimore Cooper
about a dude who REALLY identifies with Indians
while simultaneously killing a ton of Indians.
In real life, though
Custer knows almost diddly-shit about Indians
and makes up for this
by employing a ton of Indian scouts.

"INDIAN SCOUTS???" you say.
"But I thought the Indians hated white people?"
Well, there's a lot of different Indians, dorkus
and they agree with each other about as much
as a flock of seagulls trying to share a bagel.
Like, before the Europeans showed up
all the Indians were happily killing each other
for land or glory or buffalo or whatever else
when all of a sudden America showed up
with all its artillery and patriotism
and they were like "Shit
now we have to deal with this."

(This actually happened to me
the first time I played Civilization.
Abraham Lincoln just massacred me with rifles.
I never played Civilization again.)
Some tribes deal by fighting
(like the Lakota)
but some tribes deal by helping the U.S. Army
(for example, the Crow)
because they actually still hate the Lakota
plus they like fighting whoever
plus they figure if they help the U.S., they'll get land
to which I can only say
LOL.

Anyway, Custer does an excellent job
of massacring a couple defenseless villages
having sex with his captives
and staging buffalo hunts for visiting Germans
all of which has the effect
of pushing more and more tribes north
where they join this one huge village
which is right near the Little Bighorn river
and is led (sort of) by this dude named Sitting Bull.
Not only is Sitting Bull a dope-ass warrior
he's also wise as shit
like one day he goes up on a hill
and does a bunch of horrible stuff to his body
and then he passes out and wakes up
and he's like "Guys
I had a dream:
A bunch of soldiers are coming from the east
we are going to totally own them
don't take their stuff, though
that's not cool."

Sitting Bull is totally right about the soldiers
'cause Custer has heard that there is a big village

well within its treaty-defined borders
existing in a peaceful Edenic paradise
and he cannot abide by that shit
so he heads out with a big-ass army
and several other generals
all of whom are slightly less shitty than he
and when the time is right
he leaves all the other guys behind
refuses any reinforcements
and gallops off to find the giant village
BECAUSE THAT'S WHAT HEROES DO.

So Custer's Indian scouts get him to the village
but they're like "Dude, don't attack this
you will definitely die"
and Custer is like "DIE?
MORE LIKE . . . NOT DIE"
and his translators and his soldiers are like "No bro
pretty sure we will actually die if we do this"
and Custer is like "I appreciate your concerns
but I did not get this far by listening to people.
LET'S SPLIT UP, GANG
WE'LL COVER MORE GROUND THAT WAY."

So half the troops attack head-on and get slaughtered
while Custer tries to sneak around back
and also gets slaughtered
on the same hill where Sitting Bull had his dream
and all the Lakota are like "Yay!
Let's take everybody's stuff!"
and Sitting Bull is like "No wait, I said don't do that."
But no one is listening
they are too excited about not getting massacred.

So the rest of America finds out about this
and is just like ". . . What?"
Like, they can't believe that a bunch of savages

who don't even know about the Bible or trains
managed to defeat Frontier Jesus
(like American Jesus, but in buckskin!)
so they're like "I know!
Custer must have died because he WANTED TO.
SUCH NOBLE
SO SACRIFICE
WOW."
People make all these paintings about it
and write all these poems
and this dude called Buffalo Bill
who is even better than Custer
at lying about being a cowboy
even puts on a massive theatrical production of it
featuring actual Lakota battle veterans
who are willing to participate in this stupid show
because they really, really need the money.

Because here's the thing
after Custer dies
America is like "OH SHIT, PATRIOTISM"
and they fund the hell out of the army
which proceeds to wipe the floor with the Lakota
by systematically denying them food
so about half of them join reservations
and the other half (led by Sitting Bull)
move to Canada
thus continuing the time-honored American tradition
of moving to Canada every time something sucks.

But Canada sucks too, so Sitting Bull moves back
and alternates between touring with Buffalo Bill
and refusing to become a capitalist
much to the frustration of the Americans
until he eventually gets shot for "resisting arrest."
And then he's dead, and that sucks
but at least some other Indians go to school

and learn to read and write
so that future generations can better comprehend
exactly how badly they are fucked.
Also, Custer gets a monument!

So the moral of the story
is that just because someone is dead
doesn't mean they don't suck.

★ ★ ★

BILLY THE KID LOVES BACON, KILLING PEOPLE

So now that the Civil War is over
where are people gonna be violent?
I'll tell you where:
THE OLD WEST
a gleaming, steaming repository
of guns, guff, and gumption
just waiting to be covered in dead bodies.
Many people contribute to the Old West body count
but few do it more effectively
than this kid named Billy.

Billy gets born in New York City
to an Irish mom and an invisible dad.
He's a mischievous little bastard
and by the time he's like twelve
he gets a little too mischievous
and gets thrown in jail.
But it's okay
because in addition to being a mischievous bastard
he is also a little bastard, like I said
so he escapes from prison
by crawling out of the chimney
and then he goes WEST
where a mischievous little bastard like him
is bound to fit right in.

And FIT RIGHT IN HE DOES.
First he shoots a blacksmith
who's trying to push him around
then he runs off

and becomes a cattle rustler/cheesemaker
and then after doing that for a while
he gets hired by this lawyer named McSween
to GUARD some cattle
because McSween doesn't do background checks.

But maybe he did do a background check
because as a cattle guard
Billy's job description
is to basically murder all the dudes
who work for the OTHER cattle guys
who, granted, are classic mustache-twirling villains
who do things like shoot people
and then shoot their horses
and then cut off the heads of the horses
and put them on the heads of the dudes.
Messed up, I know.

So yeah, bullets fly back and forth for a while
between these two posses of bad dudes
and both sides do things that are pretty messed up
but the guys Billy is fighting against are way richer
and know way more important government dudes
and also Billy makes the mistake
of shooting at some U.S. Cavalry
so in the end, he gets indicted
and has to make a plea bargain to get a pardon
where he sells out some of his gangbros
but when he comes in to testify
THEY TOTALLY JUST ARREST HIM
so he's just like "Psh
you clearly have not heard about me and chimneys."
Then he climbs out the chimney
and rides away on a horse someone brought for him.

So now Billy the Kid is widely known
as a seriously bad dude

and the governor of New Mexico
starts offering a really sweet reward for his arrest:
FIVE HUNDRED BUCKS.
DUDE.
Five hundred bucks?!
That's barely enough to buy five hours
with a medium-classy prostitute . . .
Wait, okay, I see how this could work.

ENTER PAT GARRETT
he's a buffalo hunter
but that doesn't mean he cannot also hunt DUDES.
Dudes are basically the same as buffalo
except with less legs and more bullets.
Some say that Pat and Billy used to be best pals
but normally you do not form a posse
to go arrest/kill your best pal
for a measly five hundred bucks.
Usually it takes like six hundred at LEAST.

Anyway, Pat chases Billy around for a while
while Billy is rustling cattle HARDCORE
and also pranking dudes with his guns
like this one time
when he's hanging out in a bar
this drunk jerk is like
"I AM TOTALLY GONNA KILL BILLY THE KID."
Totally unaware of the fact that Billy
is RIGHT THERE IN THE BAR.
So Billy walks up to him
and he's like "Nice gun. Mind if I take a look?"
So the guy gives him the gun
LIKE AN IDIOT
and then instead of just shooting the dude with it
like a normal badass
Billy goes ahead and rotates the barrel
so that the next chamber to fire will be empty

and then gives it back to him
and then he's like "Oh, by the way
I'm Billy the Kid."
And the guy is like "WHAAAAAAT"
and starts shooting at him
but no bullets come out of his gun, obviously
so then Billy kills him
and everyone is like "Well, that was unnecessary
and therefore TOTALLY AWESOME."

But all awesome things must come to an end.
One morning, Pat Garrett tracks Billy and his gang
to a little house on the prairie
and he barricades the door with a dead horse
and then he starts cooking BACON.
And he's like "Hey, Billy
how would you like to come eat some tasty bacon?"
And Billy is like "Hey, Pat
how would you like to GO TO HELL?"
And Pat is like "Well, I'm sorry you feel that way
I guess you can just starve to death inside that house."
But no one can withstand the smell of bacon for long
so eventually Billy and his gang surrender
so they can get some breakfast.

Then Billy gets convicted, of course
for a whole bunch of murders
some of which he probably didn't even commit
but that's okay
because the number of murders he's accused of
makes him a TOTAL CELEBRITY.
He gets to go to Las Vegas and do interviews!
Granted, he spends a good portion of the interviews
denying a lot of those very same murders
but whatever, he's famous!
Less fortunately
it also means that he gets sentenced to death

and the prison where he's being kept in the meantime
DOESN'T EVEN HAVE A CHIMNEY.
So I guess he's just boned, right?

WRONG.
Because this is when Billy the Kid
pulls some straight-up action hero shit
like, his guards are walking him over to get executed
and he KNOCKS ONE OUT
WITH HIS MANACLES
then he steals that dude's gun
and shoots the other one in the face
after addressing him with a catchy one-liner
BY NAME.
He then has to put off his escape for an hour
while he chews through his leg irons.

But there is a natural law in the Old West.
It is called the Conservation of Gumption.
It states that one man
cannot hog all of the gumption for too long
before he has to die and let other people have a turn
and that's why
three months later
Pat Garrett finally catches up with Billy
in some random house one night
and Billy goes down like a clown
from a bullet to the stomach
while yelling "Who's there?" in Spanish.

At the time of his death
Billy is just shy of twenty-one years old
and according to some (wildly inaccurate) estimates
he has killed TWENTY-ONE MEN.
Dude
21:1 is a pretty good kill–death ratio
and even if he only killed like five guys

dude has some serious work ethic.
I mean, I've already lived longer than he did
and I have yet to kill anything
other than a spider and a couple goldfish.
Oh well
to each his own.

The moral of the story
is that if you're considering a career in murder
probably just drop it.
You're already way behind
and it'd be hell to catch up.

★ ★ ★

Pecos Bill Kicks Meteorology in the Face

So there are all these real cowboys in the Wild West
and they are all idolizing this fictional cowboy
called Pecos Bill ·
which is a problem
because Pecos Bill is an idiot.

Let's gloss right over his troubled childhood
in which he fell out of a wagon
got adopted by coyotes
and failed to realize he was not one of them
until his brother came along and told him so.
Instead, let's fast-forward to him at twentysomething
when he is acutely aware that he is not a coyote
but also acutely unaware
of certain basic facts of physics.

Like for example:
YOU CAN'T RIDE A TORNADO LIKE A HORSE.
TORNADOES DIFFER FROM HORSES
IN MANY DISTINCT WAYS.
SCIENCE HAS SHOWN THIS.

So Pecos Bill is up in Kansas for some reason
and he is like "Hey
you know what would be great to ride right now?
A FUCKING TORNADO."
So he hangs out in tornado country for a while
checkin' out the tornadoes.

He even lets a couple pass by unmolested
because they are simply not dangerous enough
but finally he sees this one tornado
tearing the bajeezus out of EVERYTHING
EVERYWHERE
turning the sky black and green
and he is like "Phew
I was worried
that I wasn't going to get to do a dumb thing today."

So Pecos Bill jumps on that tornado
pushes it to the ground
jumps on its . . . back?
and is like "Giddy up, you son of a bitch."
So the tornado
obviously
is like "FIGGITY FUCK NO."
This is not just me injecting swears into mythology
(for once)
the tornado seriously starts cursing.
Bill has pissed off this force of nature SO MUCH
it has miraculously gained the power of speech
and it is using it to say "fuck" a lot.

So the tornado flips out
(like, more than normal)
and starts tearing even more bajeezus out of things
tying rivers in knots and skull-fucking forests
killing thousands of animals
destroying vast swaths of land.
Then they get to Texas
which is pretty destroyed already because Texans
and Pecos Bill is still chilling out on this tornado
just occasionally digging his spurs into it.
I don't know what he found to dig his spurs into
but whatever it is it sure pisses the tornado off
so finally the tornado is like "Aww, Jesus fuck

no matter what I do
this asshole just keeps sitting on me
occasionally making cowboy or wolf noises
this is horrible
life is horrible
why me?"

So the tornado decides to commit suicide.
It flies over to the Grand Canyon
and cries itself out of existence
raining so hard it fills up the entire canyon
and as a result of this elemental emogasm
Pecos Bill finds himself with nothing to ride
and he flies through the air
and hits the ground so hard
it creates Death Valley
and then a bunch of cowboys are like
whoa that looks pretty sweet
let's make that a sport
only let's do it with horses instead of tornadoes
because we are stupid enough to think this looks fun
but we're not THAT stupid.
AND THAT'S WHERE RODEO COMES FROM.

So the moral of the story is
dismantle FEMA.
Pecos Bill could have stopped Katrina single-handed
or maybe made it like
a thousand times worse
in fact probably that is the more likely scenario
seeing as he devastated like 50 percent of America
so the real moral of the story is
stay the hell away from tornadoes
rodeo has already been invented
you have nothing left to gain.

Calamity Jane Has the Best Nickname

So in the Wild West
there's a couple ways to get famous:
You can kill a bunch of white dudes
you can kill a bunch of Native Americans
or you can find a bunch of gold
(and probably kill a bunch of dudes to keep it).
In this way
the Wild West is an equal-opportunity employer
they don't care if you're a man, woman, or kid
all that matters is that you have guns
and that you shower as little as possible.
Calamity Jane is proof of this.
I mean, she's pretty isolated proof of this
so either she's like the only lady who figured it out
or the Old West is not as equal-opportunity as I said
but, uh . . .
yay, cowboys!

So Martha Jane Cannery
(her non-awesome non-frontier name)
gets born in Missouri
and then her parents die
for vague, fairy-tale reasons
and suddenly Martha is the boss of all her sisters
(pro tip:
it is way easier to be a badass lady in the Old West
if your dad is dead).

So Martha moves her family from Virginia City
(which is in Montana because settlers are dumb)

all the way to Wyoming
and along the way she hangs out with all the dudes
firing pistols constantly
and riding her horse across dangerous rivers for fun
and by the time they get to Piedmont
everyone knows she bad.

So she works whatever jobs she can
mostly boring shit like washing dishes
and cooking meals and being a prostitute
and she's like "Wait a second
why am I doing this
when I could be KILLING PEOPLE?"
So she loads up a couple of guns
gets hella drunk
and proceeds to remain armed and tipsy
for most of the rest of her natural life.

Now, the frontier is a lot like Burning Man:
It's hot
it's dry
everybody's drunk
and everybody's got a goddamn nickname
except instead of techno-hippy shit
like "Alice in Wonderland" or "Love Laser"
you get random violence words
like CALAMITY JANE.
Jane says a military guy gave her the name
after she saved his life from some Indians
but I prefer to think she got it
by just being a walking talking crisis her whole life.

Anyway, she works for the military for a while
scouting and shooting and hanging with Custer a bit
(maybe
it is possible that she lied about that
when she dictated her autobiography for cash

but lying is manly too so don't worry about it)
and eventually she hooks up with another badass
called Wild Bill Hickok.

Now, Wild Bill is a character in his own right
he killed a bear in hand-to-hand combat
INVENTED the quick-draw duel
and was so stupidly lucky
he made an actual PROFESSION out of gambling.
So when Wild Bill and Calamity Jane get to town
(the town of Deadwood, South Dakota
which is so crawling with famous Western heroes
that they eventually make a TV show out of it)
what do you think the newspaper headlines say?
"NEWS FLASH:
CALAMITY JANE HAS ARRIVED."
HAHA, SCREW YOU, WILD BILL.

So Jane and Bill hang out in Deadwood for a bit
drinking and gambling
gambling and drinking
until Wild Bill gambles a little too hard
and gets shot for it
and Jane responds
by attacking the guy who did it with a meat cleaver
and then settling down to drink herself dead.
This works really well
although she does live long enough
to nurse people through a smallpox epidemic
which she is apparently immune to
due to a persistent lack of showers
and the antiseptic properties of rye whiskey.

But she finally does die
after getting thrown off a train for being drunk
and the rest, as they say, is history.
I mean, that part was history too

but I'm talking about
like
other history.

So you may be saying to yourself
"I get that Calamity Jane's ass
was about as maximally bad as an ass can be
but did she actually . . . do anything?"
Well, yes and no.
Like, she must have done something to gain her cred
but most of what we know about her
is stuff she just straight-up told her biographer
without anything to back it up
so, just like with a lot of Old West badasses
it's pretty hard to separate her real life
from the shit people made up about her
which just goes to show
that it is always better to talk the talk
than to walk the walk
because talk is way cheaper.

JOHNNY APPLESEED IS THE DELICIOUS KIND OF CRAZY

So America, right?
It has all these trees everywhere
but most of them suck
(this is two hundred years ago by the way
today I feel like we have significantly fewer trees
but I'm not sure what percentage of them suck).
We got all these like
cedar trees
pine trees
weeping willows
what the nuts, you guys
weeping willows??
I'm supposed to feel sorry for a tree
that does nothing but weep all day?
What do you have to cry about, barky?
You're a TREE
GET A JOB.

But what we don't have at all
are FREE FOOD TREES.
There are hungry dudes all over America
just DREAMING of free food trees
boughs laden with bacon and waffles
cigarettes and whiskey.
(Most of these hungry dudes are homeless, btw.
Like, have you ever listened to the song
"The Big Rock Candy Mountain"
like REALLY listened to it?
It's a song for homeless dudes, straight up.)

ENTER JOHNNY APPLESEED.
This is a dude
who for FORTY-NINE YEARS
dedicates his life
to kicking hunger in the nuts
with his bare feet.
He just walks around all over the place
with a big old sack of apple seeds
planting trees and taking names
names of people who need to be FED
and then FEEDING THEM APPLES.
He wears a pot on his head instead of a hat
and this is super convenient
because what other kind of hat can you make soup in
other than a souphat
and can someone please tell me
where can I get a souphat?
also what is a souphat?
Anyway, this dude's feet are SO TOUGH

that one time a rattlesnake tries to bite him in the foot
and it just cannot pierce the rhinoceros hide
that passes for Johnny Appleseed's foot skin
also when he gets bored he CHILLS WITH BEARS.

Native Americans totally dig this dude
I mean, what's not to like?
"Here comes that white dude with no shoes
wearing a pot on his head
handing out apples.
Do you think he might be crazy?
Who gives a shit
at least he's not setting us on fire
or taking our land."
So even when all the tribes start murdering pioneers
(because pioneers are reliably huge bastards)
they leave Johnny Appleseed alone
which he views as a perfect opportunity
to warn the settlers when there are Indians coming
at one point he runs twenty-six miles to do this.
TWENTY-SIX MILES, MY FRIENDS.
That is only three hundred yards short of a marathon.
If you were wondering
why Paul Revere doesn't have a chapter in this book
it's because Johnny Appleseed BEAT HIM HERE.
Anyway Johnny does that
and thousands more Indians die because of it
so good job Johnny Appleseed?
But mainly he just plants apple trees.

The moral of the story
is that if an apple tree falls in the forest
and there's no one around to hear it
who gives a shit?
Dude planted like a million of those.

★ ★ ★

H. H. HOLMES: THE ORIGINAL TRIPLE H

Yes, of course we have to do a serial killer
'cause if there's one constant in America
it's reverence for dudes who kill tons of people.
You can do it in war if you want
but you'll get just as much publicity
if you do it in a murder castle.

"MURDER CASTLE?" you cry
"THAT SOUNDS BITCHIN'!"
Well, it's only bitchin' if you're not inside of it
but yeah, that's why I picked the guy I picked:
DR. H. H. HOLMES
PROUD AMERICAN PIONEER
OF KILLING DEFENSELESS PEOPLE.

I mean yeah, John Wayne Gacy is terrible
what with the kid-murdering
and the side-gig as a clown
and having the name of a movie star cowboy
and Ed Gein and Ed Kemper are fine
if you like dudes named Ed.
But of all those proud soulless soldiers
who captured the public's fancy
by murdering a significant percentage of the
     public
only H. H. Holmes
the very first American serial killer
has a FUCKING MURDER CASTLE.

Ol' H-bomb starts small
by which I mean "in medical school"
where he makes money by stealing cadavers
taking out insurance policies on them
then making them look like they died by accident.
Apparently the biggest problem with this scheme
is that Holmes doesn't get to kill the cadavers himself
so once he graduates med school
he moves to Chicago
buys an empty lot
and builds a hotel
right down the street
from the proposed site of the 1893 WORLD'S FAIR
(commemorating the 400th anniversary
of when Columbus showed up in America
and killed a bunch of people for money and laughs
so if you think about it
Holmes is really just carrying on the tradition).
Oh dang, did I say he builds a hotel?
I meant to say MURDER CASTLE.

What is a murder castle, you ask?
Well, let me give you the grand tour.
On the first floor we have a drugstore
nothing to see here
and on the second and third floors . . .
we have a labyrinthine network of dead-end rooms
stairways to nowhere
and random gas vents
ready to asphyxiate you
or set you on fire
or get torn out of the wall and banged on your head.
The murder castle is not choosy about its methods.

Holmes changes builders a bunch of times
just so no one but him will know the layout

which is sort of like what Egyptian pharaohs did
except the bodies in their murder castles
WERE DEAD WHEN THEY ARRIVED.
Oh, and also the basement is a crematorium.
Have fun never staying at any hotel ever again.

The whole hotel is staffed with babes
babes with LIFE INSURANCE POLICIES
which Holmes requires them to get
but which he pays for
and is the sole beneficiary of
in case, oh, I dunno
THEY DIE IN THE MURDER CASTLE??
Add on all the random tourists from the fair
and Holmes manages to rack up a TON of murders
though I doubt he has insurance policies on strangers
so why kill them?
Well, I believe the technical term is
"for the lols."

After the World's Fair, Holmes moves to Texas
where he fails to build another murder castle
but manages to get in trouble for stealing a horse
which I guess he isn't as good at
so he runs from state to state for a while
(this is apparently before you could like
call ahead about people)
then hits up an old bro of his
one of the carpenters who helped with the castle
and is like "Hey, bro, it's me, Holmes"
and his bro Ben is like "Wassup, Holmes?"
and Holmes is like "I have a great idea:
fake your own death and collect life insurance"
and Ben is like "That's brilliant!"
and Holmes is like "Psyche, actually killing you!
Hey, Ben's wife?"

and Ben's wife is like "Yeah?"
and Holmes is like "Ben is uh . . . in London.
Can I have your kids?"
and Ben's wife is like "Sure, you seem legit."
So then Holmes kills three of her kids
for basically no reason.

But the problem with killing so many people
other than that you're killing so many people
is that you have to hide all their dead bodies.
Holmes is really good at this
but he finally fucks up
by only MOSTLY burning up one of the kids
and the cops find it
right after they arrest him for horse-stealing
right BEFORE he escapes into Canada
and once they have him in custody they're like "Hm.
We can tell you're a bad dude
but all we have is this horse thief nonsense
and like, part of a dead kid.
OH WAIT
MURDER CASTLE."

So yeah, they find the murder castle in Chicago
which pretty much seals Holmes's fate
by which I mean his death
but also his killer rep
and he spends the rest of his short life
lying ceaselessly about his murders.
Not in a constructive way, like "I didn't do it"
but in a totally random way
like "I killed twenty-seven people
no wait, two
no wait, two hundred
can we all just agree I killed people and move on?"
and everyone is like "YES.

If by move on, you mean hang you to death."
And he's like "Yeah, okay, fair enough."

So that's what they do
and everyone learns a valuable lesson:
DON'T GO INTO A MURDER CASTLE.

★ ★ ★

Susan B. Anthony Sells Out for Equality

So at around the time of the Civil War
there's all these women
seriously, tons of them
like, I kid you not
50 percent of the people in America are females
and all these ladies have one thing in common:
They can't vote
or control their own lives in any meaningful way
it's sort of a big deal for them, they are upset.
They are not alone in this predicament
slaves are also getting a pretty raw deal
(in fact I think slavery is the definition of a raw deal)
so naturally a bunch of women feel for the slaves
and since women can at least move around freely
(sort of
sometimes)
a lot of them start giving speeches and stuff
to try and stop this whole slavery thing.

Then the Civil War happens
and Abe Lincoln kicks slavery in the nuts
but guess what?
WOMEN STILL CAN'T VOTE
in fact, sometimes
they even get assed out of talking
at ANTI-SLAVERY CONVENTIONS.
So some understandably pissed-off ladies
including Lucretia Mott and Elizabeth Cady Stanton
are like "Wow, screw this."

They have a big meeting with a lot of women
where they make a list
of everything sucky that women have to deal with
(it is a long list)
and then they sign it
and then they are like "Hey
government
man up and fix this shit already."

But the government is already totally manned up
like, 100 percent men in this government right
    now
both parties are total sausage fests
so they ignore the hysterics of these women
and go about the noble manly business
of stealing land from Indians
and calling them Indians.

Luckily, getting stuff from the U.S. government
is a lot like getting stuff from your parents as a kid
except there are three parents, and they are all dads.
See, there's the legislative branch, which makes laws
(and is who the ladies originally went after)
the executive branch, which enforces the laws
(not much use if there are no good laws to enforce)
and the judicial branch, which can break shitty laws.
So when the legislature says no
Elizabeth Stanton and her pal Susan B. Anthony
decide to go to the Supreme Court
and hope that they'll say yes.

But in order to get to the Supreme Court
they have to do something illegal
and then challenge the law in court.
So in the next election
Susan B. Anthony goes down to her polling place
and she's like "Hey, guys, I wanna vote"

and they're like "You can't, 'cause of your vagina."
and she's like "Okay, I'm gonna sue the shit out of you"
and they're like "Whoa, fine, vote then"
so she's like "Woo, I get to vote!"
but she's also like "Dammit, I don't get to sue."
Luckily, the police find out a week later
and send a dude to arrest her
but she is so goddamn dignified
he almost can't even do it
and when he finally does do it
he's really wimpy and half-assed about it
and then the trial doesn't go the way she wants it to
mostly because the judge is a sly asshole.

But another woman does get to the Supreme Court.
(Hurray!)
But the Supreme Court tells her to go fuck herself
(Boo!)
and what's worse
the way they do it
is by saying that voting is not a guaranteed right
so the whole South
which at this point has JUST freed all its slaves
is like "What's that you say?
We don't have to let black people vote?
AWESOME."
So that backfires super hard.

But these dames are not about to quit.
Elizabeth Stanton goes back to Congress
and introduces a constitutional amendment
that's just like "women get to vote now"
and everyone in Congress is like "HA HA HA HA
BITCHES, AM I RIGHT?"
But Liz does not give a fuck
she just reintroduces that amendment to Congress
every year

FOR FORTY-FIVE YEARS
(actually she's dead for the last sixteen years of that
but I like to think her ghost had a hand in it).

Meanwhile, Susan B. Anthony is working HARD
traveling all across the nation
telling every single woman she meets
to support women's right to vote.
She rides trains to the north, south, east, and west
she rides trains till she has the schedules memorized
And she gets FAMOUS.

But there's drama.
See, in order to build a big women's coalition
Susan B. Anthony has to strip down her plan
from "get women all the rights they're missing"
to "get women the vote and fuck everything else."
So she starts recruiting sucky women that she hates
like racists and religious fundamentalists
and Liz Stanton is like "I'm sick of this bullshit
you can keep your organization of jerks
I'm retiring."

But when Elizabeth says "retiring"
what she actually means is
"writing a feminist revision of the Bible"
so like, a PRETTY DIFFERENT BIBLE
and all Susan's shitty friends are like "Whoa, what?
That bitch is way out of line
we need to officially declare that she sucks"
and Susan is like "Hey, guys, she's my friend"
and the jerks are like "Which would you rather have:
friendship or women's suffrage?"
and if this was an eighties movie
she would've probably gone with friendship
but this is not the eighties, it is the nineties
the *1890s*

so she's like "Ugh, suffrage I guess"
and Elizabeth totally thinks she's a sellout for that
but what are you gonna do?

This goes on for many more years
with Susan making more and more compromises
and Elizabeth becoming more and more radical
(in every sense of the word)
until finally they both die
and then sixteen years later
women finally get to vote!
It comes down to one deciding vote
by a dude from Tennessee
who only votes for the bill
because his mom told him to do it
which begs the question
where were all the other guys' moms the whole time?

So the moral of the story
is that we should keep in closer touch with our moms
because apparently they have good ideas
sometimes
I guess.

* * *

TEDDY ROOSEVELT.
THAT IS ALL.

It's okay, friend
I don't blame you
for skipping directly to this chapter
because who wants to read regular American history
when you can read about TEDDY ROOSEVELT
the only U.S. president
WITH A TYPE OF BEAR NAMED AFTER HIM.
See, when it comes to war gods
there's a couple types.
There's your cunning planners
like Athena and Odin and whatnot
and there's CRAZYBALLS BATTLECRUSHERS
like Thor and Ares and Thor's left nut.
Teddy Roosevelt is all of these things
plus a side order of King Solomon
throat-punching poverty
and altering geography
from the center of a bacon double-cheeseburger.
I don't know how that cheeseburger got in there.
Don't write myths when you're hungry.

But let's not get ahead of ourselves.
T-Rose has to grow up before he can stomp ass
and as a child, he is sickly like the Tiniest of Tims
all coughing and having asthma like a chump
so what does he do?
Does he curl up with an inhaler and make do?
NO.
He's like "FUCK LUNGS, I'M A ROOSEVELT"

and climbs mountains until asthma gives up on him.
Then he starts doing POLITICS.

But politics isn't violent enough for him
so after spending some time in charge of the navy
he peaces out to the frontier and becomes a cowboy
and then when the U.S. decides to liberate Cuba
because Spain is there being a dick
he gathers up all his pals
buys them a bunch of guns and horses
and is like "Okay, guys
I know nobody asked us to go to Cuba and kill fools
but guys:
Let's go to Cuba and kill fools."
And that is exactly what they do.
They call themselves the Rough Riders
because nothing says combat mastery
like ALLITERATION.

After he gets back from war
New York is just overcome with how manly he is
so they're like "We better elect this guy governor
because if we don't he'll probably eat us."
He does such a good job messing with millionaires
that a bunch of guys are like "We must stop him
by putting him in a position where he can't harm us.
Oh, how about vice president?
Vice presidents don't do diddly."

Joke's on them though
because after the election, President McKinley dies
(actually the joke is on President McKinley
if you consider a lone anarchist's bullet to be a joke
which I totally do because I have no soul)
and now Roosevelt is president.
So Teddy's like "BOOYAH, I'M ON THIS.
Okay, guys, there are a few things I wanna change.

Let's start with . . .
EVERYTHING."
So he designates a bunch of national parks
prosecutes a bunch of big corporate monopolies
digs a canal through Panama
(after supporting a revolution in Panama just for that)
regulates railroad prices
negotiates a treaty between Russia and Japan
speaks softly
carries a BIG stick (if you know what I mean)
and changes the rules of football.
Then he has lunch.

He gets reelected until he refuses to run anymore
then he gets sick of everyone else's political crap
and decides to run again
and when the Republicans won't nominate him
he nominates HIMSELF
by starting his OWN DAMN PARTY
called the Progressive Party
oh wait I mean the BULL MOOSE party
as in what Teddy Roosevelt is as healthy as.

He does not become president
but he does accomplish something way better:
during his campaign, he's on his way to do a speech
when some jerk shoots him in the chest
like, with a gun.
The bullet goes through his steel glasses case
through a copy of his fifty-page speech
and only then does it reluctantly enter his chest.
So Teddy looks at his chest
sees that he is not coughing up blood
and is like "Eh, it's probably fine."
Then he goes ahead and speaks
for NINETY MINUTES
at which point the ghost of John Henry stands up

and starts a slow clap
which is eventually joined by EVERY VIKING.

So Teddy doesn't get to be president
but he doesn't care
because all of that politicking was distracting him
from his true passion:
risking his life to map the Brazilian jungle.
So he goes down there
contracts tropical supermalaria
finishes the expedition anyway
and then goes back home and refuses to die.

Then World War One starts happening
and he goes to the president (Woodrow Wilson)
like "Put me in, coach, put me in!"
But Wilson is like "Dude
you have tropical supermalaria
a bullet in your chest
and didn't you have asthma at one point?
Stay home, dog."
And Teddy is like "Aww . . ."
then he dies
but, like, in his sleep
because
as his friends confirm
Death could not have handled him if he was awake.

Oh, but I was gonna tell you about teddy bears.
See, back on one of his massive hunting sprees
Theodore Roosevelt came upon a black bear.
This bear was defenseless
shooting it would not have been even a little fun
so he didn't shoot it
even though all his pals were telling him to.
Some toy manufacturer found out about this
and BAM, teddy bears.

Roosevelt hated the nickname Teddy
but it totally stuck
which just goes to show
that sometimes
what matters is the things you DON'T shoot.

★ ★ ★

AL CAPONE GETS
EVERYONE HAMMERED

Okay. so there's this dude Alphonse
but that name is neither manly enough
NOR American enough
So let's call him Al
Al Capone.

Picture this:
CHICAGO IN THE 1920s
aka the single most corrupt location in space-time.
You see
there are not a lot of employment opportunities
for Italian immigrants at this time
the options are basically limited to:
1. Manual labor
2. Petty crime
3. EXTREMELY NON-PETTY CRIME
And obviously Al is not gonna half-ass his crime
so he makes friends with this gang lord
named Johnny Torrio
and Torrio calls him up one day like "Hey, bud
wanna move from New York to Chicago
to help me completely take over every illegal thing?"
And Capone is like "I'll give you a hint:
not no."

Chicago is awesome for doing crimes in
it is like a lush rain forest of crime
with each horrible person
linked inseparably to every other horrible person
by a complex and beautiful web of death:

like, politicians and cops let mobsters do whatever
then elections happen
and mobsters beat up voters
until those politicians and cops win.
It's the CIIIIRCLE OF CRIIIIIIME.

Chicago is CORRUPT
(how corrupt is it?)
it is SO CORRUPT
that Al Capone
is a DEPUTY SHERIFF
like, he's driving drunk with a bunch of hookers
he rams into a parked taxi
and then he jumps out
waving a gun and his SHERIFF'S BADGE.
GUYS:
THIS IS THE CITY WHERE I NOW LIVE.

This continues for a long time
and it could have continued even longer
with all kinds of bad dudes
making all kinds of mad money
but as we all know
the only thing better than money
is MORE money
so pretty soon dudes start dying.

See, around this time
Congress straight-up amends the constitution
to be like "No more booze for anyone.
Love, Congress."
CONGRESS:
STOP BEING SUCH A LITERAL BUZZKILL.
So a lot of gangsters
especially Johnny Torrio
are like "DUDES
BOOZE IS ILLEGAL NOW

WE CAN MAKE SO MUCH CASH SELLING IT."
But Torrio's boss
this guy Colosimo
is like "I dunno guys
selling liquor seems mighty risky
I think I'll just stick to my gambling and whores"
so Torrio is like "Dude, I know you're my uncle
but your ass needs to die"
and Colosimo is like "Oh nooooo."

So now Torrio is the head of a big crime syndicate
along with his pal Capone
and they're selling booze like hotcakes
(hotcakes that are secretly filled with booze)
so now can everybody stop dying
and start making mad cash?
NOPE
Why, you ask?
Dion O'Banion is why.

Dion O'Banion is the best gangster
he carries three guns at all times
even though he only has two hands
he makes a large portion of his money
by selling flowers to gangster funerals
and every time he does a thing
it seems to be with the explicit idea
of pissing off as many Italians as possible.

So O'Banion dies, obviously
(in his flower shop, it's way cinematic)
and all his guys are like "Awesome
we were looking for an excuse to kill everyone."
So now dudes are just shooting each other all day
every day
in the street, downtown, at like noon.
Dudes die in restaurants and bowling alleys

in the business district or wherever.
So many dudes die in barbershops
that barbers start facing the seats toward the door
just so gangsters won't be so freaked out.

It's a mess
and Capone is having none of it
so while he's vacationing in Miami
(and by "vacationing"
I mean "being questioned by the cops
as to how he got the money
to buy a house in frikkin' Miami")
he has a couple of his guys dress like cops
and go to an auto garage full of O'Banion dudes
and be like "Hey, guys, you're under arrest.
HAHA PRANKED
WE'RE ACTUALLY SHOOTING YOU."
And to this day
couples across the world celebrate this massacre
every February 14
by giving each other flowers and edible underwear.

So at this point
pretty much every single person
who could possibly oppose Capone
is dead.
He is basically the mayor of Chicago.
Dudes come to him like
"Please, Mr. Capone
could you ensure a fair and safe election?"
and Capone is like "Sure
it was me that was gonna make it unsafe anyway"
and then the election is safe
just because he said so.

And once Al owns basically all of Chicago
he can afford to be a nice dude.

He's constantly giving money to orphans and shit
buying his mom nice houses
giving whiskey to one-legged puppies
whatever
everybody loves this dude
so finally the government is like "Shit
we gotta make this guy look bad.
But how?"

The first thing they try
is they name him Public Enemy Number One.
This does not work at all
because that is an objectively rad title.
So then they hire this dude Eliot Ness
and give him a big sack of money
and they say, "Okay, dude
make Capone's life suck."

So Eliot Ness just drives around Chicago
blowing up distilleries and filming it.
But it turns out that Ness cares more about publicity
than actually doing a good job
so nothing he does actually results in a conviction
(he does get a lot of movies made about him though
and his dudes get nicknamed "The Untouchables"
which might be a better name than "Public Enemy"
but there's no rapper named "The Untouchables"
so it evens out).

So finally the government gives up being cool
and just does what it does best:
It buries Capone in paperwork.
Seriously, they spend five years
reading ALL his financial records
just to figure out how many taxes he's not paying
based on the solid idea
that just because your income is illegal

doesn't mean you can avoid paying taxes on it.
So they bust Capone for tax evasion.
The Founding Fathers would've gone to war over this
but Al Capone just goes to JAIL.
They send him to Alcatraz
which they pretty much opened just for him
and he learns to play the banjo there
but other than that it sucks.

It especially sucks because Al is sick.
Apparently a lifetime of banging whores
can saddle you with certain inconvenient diseases
like for example syphilis
which Al has repeatedly refused tests for.
BECAUSE HE'S TERRIFIED OF NEEDLES.
This dude once beat two dudes to death with a bat
and he will not have blood taken to save his life
LITERALLY.
Finally they figure it out though
around the time his brain totally stops working
and then they feel sorta bad for him
so they let him out of prison
and people pretend to respect him until he dies
of pneumonia
before the age of fifty.

So the moral of the story
is that when you're running a criminal empire
you should always use a condom.

★ ★ ★

Thomas Edison Is a Killing Machinist

Did you think I forgot about electricity?
Tsk tsk, friends
what good is a pantheon without a god of lightning?
Benjamin Franklin was all well and good
FOR A WHILE
but we needed someone to get modern with this shit
so listen up:

When last we left our heroes
they were busy proving that lightning was electric
and then going to France and having a lot of sex
and apparently all this was crucial
(especially that last part)
because it opened the door for a dude named
    Faraday
to come along and start making machines
that rubbed shit on other shit
with UNHEARD-OF EFFICIENCY.
He also invented a kind of cage
that makes your cell phone not work
so basically he sounds like a dick
BUT HE IS AN IMPORTANT DICK.
History is full of important dicks
like Alexander the Great
and Napoleon
and Benjamin Franklin's dick
but there are at least as many important ASSHOLES.
Enter Thomas Alva Edison.

See, after Faraday invents his super efficient method
for rubbing shit together
Thomas Edison gets very rich
by selling crazy souped-up telegraphs
and puts up a gigantic building in New Jersey
so that he can more efficiently gather smart people
and rub their brains together
(as a side note
I am currently pioneering a new theory of history
it is called
"everything in history as rubbing things on things")
and through the friction of all these smart brains
Edison comes up with some pretty cool ideas
or more accurately
better versions of other people's already cool ideas
like lightbulbs and whatever
and one of the things he comes up with
is another way to generate and distribute electricity.
Edison calls his way "direct current"
(or DC)
and the other way
which is being pioneered at the same time
by a dude named Westinghouse
is called "alternating current"
(or AC).
Do not try to understand what these things mean
it's really hard
all you need to know
is they would make an incredibly sweet band name.

So the problem with DC power
is it's lazy
it won't travel very far before it gives up
so you gotta make tons of power stations for it to use.
Meanwhile
the problem with AC power

is that someone has not yet come along
who can upgrade it and make it TOTALLY RAD.
ENTER NIKOLA TESLA.

Tesla is this Serbian dude with like no social skills
because he put all his stat points in CRAZY BRAIN.
He willingly gave up rubbing his junk on ladies' junk
so he could spend more time rubbing electric junk
plus he hallucinated like ALL THE TIME
because he slept like NONE OF THE TIME.
This dude was less of a dude
and more of a streamlined engine
for turning water and saltines into SCIENCE.

So Tesla looks at AC power like "Okay, guys
I see what you're doing
with the rubbing stuff on other stuff
but guys
what if we made it
MORE COMPLICATED???"
and everyone is like "AWRIIIIGHT"
especially that Westinghouse guy
so Westinghouse buys all of Tesla's great ideas
and then Edison is like "Oh man
Westinghouse is about to totally wreck my shit.
AC power can travel longer distances than DC power
and it is cheaper and more efficient . . .
Welp
I guess there's only one thing left to do:
time to start murdering animals."

THAT IS, NO JOKE, WHAT EDISON DOES.
First he invents the electric chair
and powers it with AC power
so everyone will know just how dangerous that shit is
ignoring the fact that lightning can also kill people

and I'm pretty sure that's not AC OR DC
ELECTRICITY:
JUST PRETTY DANGEROUS ALL AROUND.

But Edison doesn't stop at fixing American justice
no no no
he starts stealing stray cats
and frying those babies on his electro-kill machine
but everyone is still like yawn
so finally Edison is like "Fuck this.
Just fuck this.
I'm gonna get an elephant from the goddamn zoo
stick an electrode up its butt
and shock it to DEATH
while filming it with another of my inventions
and THAT is going to solve this whole thing for me
I don't see how it could fail."

So he kills Topsy the Elephant
and then shows people the video
and somehow
that fails to convince everyone to buy his electricity
but it's fine, because it's not like Edison is poor.
He gets distracted pretty quickly
by an ambitious scheme
to repeatedly fire X-rays into his own eyes
presumably in order to become more like Superman.

Meanwhile, things are not going too well for Tesla
because after a brilliant career of turning down ladies
and sculpting reality with his mind
said mind is finally like "Okay, I'm done
it's just gonna be martians and talking pigeons now
all day every day"
and Tesla is like "Oh well
I guess I better go die in a tiny apartment
after living on milk and crackers for months."

And once Tesla and Edison are dead
from crazy and diabetes respectively
everybody's like "You know what
why don't we just compromise?
We'll use AC to get electricity into our houses
and once it's there we'll turn it into DC
and use it to make our toast and power our dildos"
and that's why pretty much every appliance you use
needs some kind of DC converter on it
so thanks a lot, past people.

Now, guys
I know you were expecting the standard narrative
"Nikola Tesla invented radar and gravity and knees
and Thomas Edison stole all of it
with his asshole machine made of assholes"
and while Thomas Edison is indeed an asshole
and Nikola Tesla did indeed invent a million things
what both of them have in common
is being MEGA CRAZY.
Like, from my perspective
there is not a lot of difference
between hallucinating pigeons and aliens
and shooting yourself in the eyes with X-rays
which just goes to show
that all the smartest people in the world
are secretly the biggest goddamn idiots.

★ ★ ★

THE GREAT DEPRESSION
WAS ACTUALLY NOT
SO GREAT

So back in olden times
(by which I mean about a hundred years ago)
all the great economies of Europe
plus the United States of America
had mad buxx
mostly from exploiting Africa
and Asia
and South America
and North America too, if you think about it
so the combined wealth of all these continents
is mostly focused on this one little tiny continent
which only really gets to be its own continent
because back when the Greeks were naming stuff
they didn't have satellites
to tell them Asia and Europe are joined at the hip.

ANYWAY
these hella wealthy bros all worship the same god
no, not God
Nietzsche already told everybody that dude was dead
the god I am referring to is called the Gold Standard
and it has only one commandment:
The amount of money you have in your country
must equal the amount of shiny yellow metal
that your country has found in the ground.
It is a pretty arbitrary way to handle money
but so far so good
mainly because people keep finding gold in Africa

so there keeps being more money
which people are stoked about
because they never want to stop buying things.

But guess what?
WAR HAPPENS.
Yeah, some dude gets shot in Austria
he's named for the indie band that wrote "This Fire"
and I guess that band is really big in Europe
because his death makes everybody start fighting.
They call it the Great War
but it's actually a pretty sucky war for everyone.

Here's why:
War is way expensive
and nobody really budgets for it
so everybody's economic strategy becomes
"Let's just win the war
and then make the other guys pay for it."
But they still have to get the money in the meantime
so they borrow it
mostly from the United States
but also from Britain.
The U.S. gets mad rich off of this
and ends up with most of the world's gold.
But then everybody still doesn't have enough money
so what do they do?
They just print more money.
Being a government is awesome.

The war goes on for four years
and at the end of it, Germany loses
the problem being that of all the guys in the war
Germany was the MOST SURE it was gonna win
so it borrowed/made up THE MOST MONEY
and now Britain and France are like "Hey, Germany
you need to pay us back all the money we spent

you know, on killing you"
and meanwhile the U.S. is like "Oh, hi there, guys
you need to pay *us* back all the money *we* gave you
you know, to kill Germany"
and Britain and France are like "Okay, sure
just let us get all that money Germany owes us"
and Germany is like "Uhh . . .
we don't have this money."

So Germany can't pay France and Britain
and France and Britain can't pay America
because the Gold Standard says money = gold
and America already has all the gold.
But America won't forgive the loans
so Germany starts printing dumpsters full of money
just to keep up appearances
until one U.S. dollar
is worth six hundred and thirty BILLION marks.
There's so much cash, kids are building money forts
it is tragic/pimp as hell.

Britain does convince America to go easy
and lower the interest rates on the loans
but in order to do that
America has to lower ALL THE INTEREST RATES
so everybody back in the U.S. is like "SWEET
FREE MONEY
BETTER USE IT TO BUY STOCKS"
and they just go nuts
the whole stock market goes completely bonkers
shoe-shine boys are giving out hot tips
hobos have stock portfolios
and the dudes in charge are TERRIFIED
because they know that at this point
the market is just running on bullshit and dreams
and real soon it's gonna get to that part in the dream

where you're naked at your tuba recital
and you never learned to play the tuba.

There are other people who are like "NAW
THE MARKET WILL BE GREAT FOREVER
PUT ALL YOUR MONEY IN IT"
but you know what those people are?
WRONG.
WRONG LIKE A DOG EATING MAYONNAISE.
The market goes down like a clown
and a bunch of people lose a bunch of money.
It happens on a Tuesday
and everybody calls it Black Tuesday
and then it happens again on Black Thursday
also Black Monday.
Everyone is so poor
they have even pawned their creativity.

But it's still not that bad
banks are still in business and whatnot
OH WAIT, I SPOKE TOO SOON
because then some guy goes into a bank in NYC
a bank that has made a foolish promise
to buy back their own stock
at the amount it was worth when they gave it away
and the dude is like "Hey
this stock is worth a quarter of what it used to be
gimme all my money back."
And the bank is like "Uhh, are you suuure?
That stock is a reeeeally good investment
maybe you should keep it so we don't hafta
    pay you."
And the dude is like "I SEE YOUR GAME.
YOU'RE OUT OF MONEY.
HEY, EVERYBODY:
THIS BANK IS OUT OF MONEY

COME GET YOUR MONEY OUTTA THIS BANK."
And everybody does.

It turns out the bank has been being mega shady
and doesn't have nearly enough money to pay people
so it closes down
and seeing as it's one of the biggest banks in NYC
it's sort of like knocking down a domino
onto a series of other dominoes
except the dominoes are the size of skyscrapers
and are full of napalm and EVERYONE'S MONEY.

So the Federal Reserve is watching this happen
(the Federal Reserve is a bank
whose main job
is to lend money to the U.S. government
except by lend money
I mean print totally new money
and then hope the government pays it back
which it NEVER EVER DOES)
and the Fed is like "All these banks are dying
should we do something?
Maybe print them out some money
so they can pay all these people
thus averting this crisis before it destroys America?
. . . Meh."

So America gets destroyed
also the rest of the world
because remember, nobody has money.
Everybody is very sad about this
you might even call them
. . . DEPRESSED?
Seriously though, lots of people kill themselves
and the rest of them move into big tent cities
wearing patched-up clothes and eating canned beans.
It's a hipster's paradise.

But it's okay
because this is when Franklin Roosevelt shows up.
He's like "OKAY, GUYS
I KNOW NOTHING ABOUT ECONOMICS
LET'S DO THIS."
And he manages to sort of fix the Depression
basically by issuing a giant patch to capitalism:
no more gold standard.

So people read the patch notes on Capitalism 0.2
and they're all like "WTF, GOLD GOT NERFED"
and Roosevelt is like "Haha, fuck you guys
now I can make dollars as cheap as I want
and tons of money will be available
and everyone will start buying things again
CAPITALISM IS SAVED."

This . . . actually works.
In fact, everyone else in the world does it too
and that is why
to this day
when a bunch of shitty banks get the world in trouble
the Fed can just print enough money to save them
which seems to piss everybody off
but hey
it's better than eating your shoes.

So I guess the moral of the story
is that capitalism works
it's just super buggy.

★ ★ ★

FDR Doesn't Like Asians Very Much

So there's this dude Hitler
he does the world a tremendous public service
by being basically the worst person ever
thus giving us a way to calibrate our evilometers
for all future bastards and despots.
He does this by selecting a subset of German people
(white dudes with blond hair and blue eyes)
and then attempting to kill
LITERALLY EVERY OTHER PERSON.
Somehow, probably with hypnotism
he is able to convince Japan to go with him on this
AND SO BEGINS WORLD WAR TWO
(man, wouldn't it be hilarious
if someone traveled back to the 1920s
and accidentally referred to the Great War
as World War One
like ha ha!
Spoilers!).

But to start out, it's not really a world war
because you know who's not involved?
AMERICA, THAT'S WHO
(by that measure, WWI wasn't a world war either
because Asia wasn't really involved
but everybody loves a sequel).
Most people in America are happy to sit out
and let the rest of the world blow itself up
because America at this time has not yet discovered
that it is actually the world's police force.
Luckily, America has a president who does know this

FRANKLIN DELANO ROOSEVELT.
Yes, the same FDR who killed the Depression
and the same FDR who will STAY administratin'
until his brain literally explodes
and they change the constitution
so no one can ever do that shit again.
This dude serves as president for thirteen years
and this is an example
of the sort of behavior that let him set that record:

So Japan is allied with Germany
and they're like "Sweet
the rest of the world already hates us
let's take their land!"
So they start invading China
and Malaysia
and the Philippines
and just whatever else
but then they're like "Hmm
what if America tries to stop us?
Ooh! Let's surprise attack Hawaii!"

So that's exactly what they do.
The attack is very successful
but only in a strictly technical sense.
To put it in perspective, let's try a metaphor.
Let's say you're having a barbecue
but you don't want to get stung by any bees
so you find your local beehive
and just go crazy on it with a baseball bat.
Make sense?
THEN YOU MUST BE JAPAN IN THE '40s.
WHO ELSE WOULD EVER DO THIS?

So the U.S. swarms on Japan, obviously
but that's where our bee metaphor breaks down
because while bees can sting you

they cannot put you in concentration camps
(or at least, I haven't met any bees that can do that).

Yeah, after that surprise attack on Pearl Harbor
everybody on the West Coast is like "OMG
WE'RE AT WAR WITH JAPAN
AND THERE ARE JAPANESE DUDES
LIVING ALLLL AROUND US."
I mean, they already banned Japanese immigration
like a decade before
but there are still Japanese dudes all over the coast
and what's more
those Japanese dudes are living right next door
to all the important aircraft factories
and landing strips
and shipyards
and farmland
and forests
and bridges
almost as if those types of things are
EVERYWHERE
and thus impossible not to live next door to.
Whatever, it's pretty suspicious.

Now, at this point, nothing has been sabotaged
and some people think that means they're safe.
But not military geniuses like Earl Warren
who points out
that the only reason there's been no sabotage
is that the Japanese are waiting for their moment
and the fact that there has been no sabotage yet
is ALL THE PROOF WE NEED
to determine that sabotage is being planned.
Frank Roosevelt hears this
and he's like "That's some pretty shaky logic
but I really don't like Japanese people.
Okay, go ahead."

So he passes an executive order
that just says "Any enemy ex-patriots
can be kicked out of any war zone I designate.
P.S.: California, Oregon, and Washington are war zones
have fun with that."
So they kick all the Japanese off the coast
forcing them to sell everything they own
but people are still not satisfied.
They're like "Those guys look funny!
We can't have funny-looking dudes roaming around
this is wartime!
We gotta lock 'em up."
And FDR is like "Okay, sure."

So they herd all the Japanese into big *camps*
where they are *concentrated* in large numbers
like a hundred and ten thousand people total
and then the military is like "Okay, guys
we will let you go
if you fill out this loyalty questionnaire
that says you love the United States
and are totally down to be in our army"
and some dudes are like "Sweet, free release!"
but some dudes are like "Seriously?
You just put me in jail for being Asian.
This country is just one giant asshole
and it's squatting directly over my head."
And the military is like "Ooh, sorry to hear that buddy
looks like you're gonna stay here for the whole war.
Meanwhile your friends get to go fight and die
FOR FREEDOM."

Some dudes go to court about this
and the cases get all the way to the Supreme Court
who are just like "Sorry guys, our hands are tied"
and all the Japanese are like "Really?"
and the Supreme Court is like "Really

as in we are being denied crucial information
that would prove that you guys aren't a threat at all
and make the military look hella foolish.
This is what happens
when you elect a general your first president
and then constantly fight wars for 150 years:
the army starts to get out of hand."
and the Japanese are like "Okay, I guess we understand
NO, WAIT, FUCK YOU GUYS."
And the Supreme Court is like "HAHA
FUCK *YOU.*
JUSTICE, BITCHES."
Then they fly away with their magic robes.

The good news is that the war ends pretty fast.
It turns out that pissing off a huge neutral party
that has been constantly fighting wars for 150 years
is not a great way to win wars
so the Japanese get to go home eventually
but they're none too happy about it
until later, when Jimmy Carter becomes president
and he decides that the whole thing was a mistake
and gives $20,000 to every camp survivor!
Sweet deal!

Which brings us to our moral:
If you're down on your luck
just have your entire race subjugated
by a country that prides itself on equality.
It's a great way to get rich quick
or, you know, eventually.

★ ★ ★

Superman Is the Definition of an Illegal Alien

So while some people are busy making history
which they hope will eventually become mythology
a group of shrewd young entrepreneurs
discover that it's possible
to skip straight to mythology
through the simple expedient
of drawing a bunch of very muscular people
in very tight clothing.
These muscular people are called "superheroes"
and they are like ancient heroes in many ways:
They are capable of incredible feats
they have impossibly sexy bodies
and they are born in nonstandard ways.
EXAMPLE:
SUPERMAN.

So there's this planet full of superheroes
and it's going to explode
You'd think that if they were so great
they would have figured out a way to not explode
but you shouldn't complain
because their loss is our gain
in the form of SUPERMAN.

Okay, actually he's not called Superman yet
that would be silly on a planet full of super people

except I don't think they have powers there
because their powers require Earth's yellow sun
and their sun is green or some other dumb color.
But anyway I guess baby Superman is important
(he's named Kal-El though
in honor of Nicolas Cage's son)
so his parents put him on a rocket ship
and shoot him toward a planet
because that's what you do with babies?

This planet they send him to
has a pretty good track record
of hating anyone even remotely different
and expressing this hatred
with stuff like witch trials.
Yes, I'm talking about Earth
specifically the America part of Earth
and Superman arrives JUST IN TIME
for the beginning of World War Two.
It's sort of a terrible introduction to Earth culture.

So Superman crashes his space raft
in the middle of the most xenophobic part of Kansas
and he gets picked up by these two old people
and they don't want to piss off the freaky space baby
so they make it their own
and anyway I think they both have cancer now
or are at least sterile from radiation poisoning
because the spaceship Superman crashed in
is like COVERED in kryptonite
which Superman is totally allergic to
so bad luck, huh?

But anyway they raise him
and teach him solid American values
like honest sweat and war and heterosexuality

and they eventually figure out shit is fucked up
when he starts lifting tractors
but by then it's too late to do anything about it
without getting hit with a flying tractor.

So Supes gets bored of his shitty podunk parents
kicks the shit out of his high school
and flies to Mars or New York or something
and gets a job as a dude who . . .
writes newspaper articles?
Because if you're an invincible force for good
with the capacity to save ANYONE at ANY TIME
what you really need to be doing
is wasting time writing about the Kardashians
and hitting on your coworkers.
But he still does save a lot of people /
shoot a lot of people with laser vision
also he can fly.

The U.S. finally decides to enter World War Two
and Superman takes some time off journalism
to just punch Nazis for a decade
but then he runs out of Nazis to punch
and he uses his influence as Best Hero Ever
to create a high council of more interesting heroes
like Batman and the Flash and Wonder Woman.
This council is not democratically elected
admission is granted based solely on genetics
(although to be fair, Batman doesn't have powers
he just buys his way in with his *immense wealth*)
They are not accountable to any higher authority
and most of the members are not even human.
As a matter of fact
when Superman's arch-nemesis becomes president
Superman goes to the oval office and KILLS HIM
starting a worldwide nuclear catastrophe

which his friends have to fix using time travel.
God bless America.

The moral of the story
is that if you wear a lot of red and blue on your body
people will just assume whatever you do is patriotic.

★ ★ ★

ELVIS LIVES!

Still not convinced that America has a mythology?
EAT COUNTEREXAMPLE, DOUBTERS.
This counterexample is from the 1950s
and is named ELVIS PRESLEY.
This guy is equal parts Orpheus
Dionysus
and Hercules.
(Don't worry, it'll all make sense by the end.)

Like all great heroes, his family is super poor
but when he is still a wee lad
his family somehow scrapes together enough cash
to get him his first guitar
which he is actually pretty disappointed about
but only because what he really wanted was a GUN
and how American is that?
Still, he gets the guitar
and I cannot for the life of me figure out why
but he keeps practicing
even when everyone he runs up on
seems intent on finding ever more creative
    ways
to tell him how bad he sucks.
Like, if I had a nickel
for every dude who told young Elvis he couldn't sing
well, I'd still be nowhere near as wealthy as Elvis
especially when you factor in inflation
but I'd have a lot of nickels
which I could put in a sock and hit people with
and in the end, isn't that what really matters?

But young Elvis don't care.
He just keeps on losing singing contests
and styling his hair with Vaseline and antigravity
until one day he struts into this record studio
and he gets DISCOVERED.

Now, there is a reason why this happens
and it's a pretty racist reason.
See, at this time in ancient American history
white people and black people are not on great terms
especially in the South, where Elvis lives.
Black people can't even see a white CONCERT
and vice versa.
But there are a bunch of white dudes
who REALLY dig the music black people are making.
They just wish it was a white guy singing it, is all
and along comes Elvis
who grew up listening to this music
and has, like, the PERFECT VOICE for it
so the white dudes who own the record label are like
"All right
we can make this work."

AND MAKE IT WORK THEY DO.
And they also make MANY DOLLARS
and not only that
but when Elvis starts doing concerts
it turns out that he is also SUPER SEXY
like, he starts waggling his hips
because he is actually pretty nervous
but it turns out that with every waggle of his hips
he is also waggling the heartstrings
of EVERY LADY IN THE ROOM.
He waggles their heartstrings so hard
that they start throwing their g-strings at him
and then make him autograph their sexyparts
which, in the 1950s, is anything above the ankle.

So of course he keeps doing these hip-waggles.
In fact, he starts waggling his hips EVEN MORE
and some people don't approve of this waggling
like devout Christians and stuff
which is funny, because Elvis is also super Christian
he's just a Christian who likes to waggle.

But all the anti-wagglers in the world
can't stop Elvis
who gets super rich and well-known
and starts being in movies and stuff
until DISASTER STRIKES:
Elvis Presley gets drafted into the U.S. ARMY.
He's fine with that, though
because he is a GODDAMN AMERICAN HERO.
So he gets shipped over to Germany for a while
and every time he goes on leave
he records like a million top-selling records
and meanwhile he uses all of his crazy riches
to buy all kinds of swag for his army buddies
like new fatigues, and color TVs, and amphetamines.
He also manages to not get killed, which is good.

Then he comes back home
and wastes seven years on terrible music/movies
until finally he's like "Wait a second . . .
Didn't I used to be a total badass or something?"
At which point he puts on a white sequined jumpsuit
rivaling the combined glory of Zeus and Ramses
and he does him some CONCERTS.

I'm sorry, did I say SOME concerts?
I meant ALL the concerts.
This guy is pulling off like 170 concerts a year!
That is too many concerts!
And as if that wasn't enough
he is also constantly improving his crazy mansion

(Graceland)
which is located at
3764 Elvis Presley Boulevard in Memphis, Tennessee.
Wait
how is ELVIS FUCKING PRESLEY number 3764
on the street that BEARS HIS NAME??
Well, whatever.
The point is that it's a modern-day pleasure palace
complete with plush purple drapes
an indoor waterfall
and limitless hamburgers.

Elvis likes to sit in the basement
watching three TVs at once
changing channels by shooting TVs WITH GUNS.
CHANNEL SURFING WITH GUNS:
THE MOST AMERICAN ACTIVITY THERE IS.
And as if THAT wasn't enough
Elvis also gets wayyy into KARATE.
Yeah, he starts learning all these deadly moves
and jumping around and doing karate chops on stage
and at one point
some dudes try to bum-rush him
during a show
and he BEATS THE SHIT OUT OF THEM
BY HIMSELF.
(Also one of his wives bangs her karate instructor
so there's that.)

But he's doing WAY TOO MANY concerts/drugs.
He's only about forty
but he is on so many drugs
that his age is effectively doubled.
His circulatory system is like that party house
where everyone went when you were in college
the one where they never had time to clean the vomit
because of too many parties.

You know what I'm talking about.
Well, even if you don't, I'm sure Elvis would have.
He's just stumbling up to the mic at this point
holding on for dear life
slurring his words
like he's giving a drunken blowjob to a horse.
It's not pretty
nobody likes it
and his audiences are getting less and less sexy too.
So after selling over seventy-five million records
and topping even more charts with his albums
than with his blood-toxicity levels
Elvis finally goes down.
He dies on the floor of his bathroom in Graceland
with about fifteen different drugs in his system
which is pretty legendary on its own.
But what happens afterward is even more legendary.

So you remember Hercules, right?
You remember how he died
after a long and storied career
because his wife gave him POISON?
But then he didn't really die
because the gods took pity on him
and put him in SPACE??
Yeah, I think you know where this is going.
Because Elvis may have died of a drug overdose
but he was such a radical musician
that ALIENS took pity on him
and put him
(say it with me now)
INNNNNNNN SPAAAAAAACE.

And to this day, his worshipers perform his rites
dressing in his traditional garb
reenacting his greatest achievements
holding massive conventions in his name every year

saying prayers and bringing offerings
to his final resting place
in the meditation garden at Graceland.
And on top of that
on top of ALL THAT
there's his name
which is
(say it with me now)
THE KING.
QED, BITCHES.

★ ★ ★

J. ROBERT OPPENHEIMER IS THE GOD OF GUNS

So this war is going on, right?

What am I saying
there's ALWAYS a war going on
but guys
I swear this war is different
because World War Two
is a war
TO END ALL WARS.
Now, granted
fighting a war to end all wars
is sort of like
eating a cyanide burger to end all meals
but it's the thought that counts.
The thought, and also the dead bodies.

But this war has been going on for a WHILE
and everyone's pretty ready for it to stop
and then some scientists are like "Hey
if you want, we can just make a really big bomb
like, REALLY big
like, big enough to just delete cities
to the point where war is meaningless
and we are all left to contemplate our decisions"
and Germany
who has already put the pedal to the metal
as far as morally questionable decisions go
is like "SHIT YEAH, HUGE BOMBS."

So the U.S. figures out that Germany is doing this
and they're like "Wow
Germany is basically a big bag of psychos
if they get this bomb
and no one else has it
they will nuke the entire goddamn world
they might even nuke the moon
there's no telling with those guys.
Should we stop them?
... Nah
let's just make our own."

So they make a super secret laboratory
out in a part of New Mexico no one cares about
and they buy a bunch of uranium from Britain
and they get
to
work.
Some of the companies that are supplying them
like DuPont and Standard Oil
and everybody else that liberals hate
are being investigated at this time
for antitrust violations
but NOW IS NOT THE TIME TO INVESTIGATE
WE HAVE TO BUILD A SUPERWEAPON.
So all those antitrust suits get suspended
and these megacorps just get to keep on monetizin'
all so we can build a mass-murder tool more quickly
which is right up there
with making deals with the actual Devil
in terms of major red flags about your goals.

Anyway there are all these scientists
stuck way out in the New Mexico desert
under the management of a guy named Oppenheimer
and everybody's sort of like "Uhh

are we sure we're doing the right thing?
Eh, whatever."
And then they invent this bomb
and they set it off
even though they think it MIGHT end the world
and the explosion
is
AWESOME.

Now, this part is critical
this explosion
is probably the most important moment
in modern mythology
because when Doc Opp sees that explosion
devouring the New Mexican dawn
he looks deep inside himself and he says
"I have become death, destroyer of worlds."
That's a quote from the Bhagavad Gita, fyi
and the dude who originally says it is Shiva
ACTUAL GOD OF DEATH.
What I am saying, guys
is that when that bomb exploded in Los Alamos
that was the moment the old gods died
and the new gods were born.
From that point to today, we've been on our own.
All that wild shit God did in the Old Testament?
That's us now
and we are EXACTLY AS IMMATURE as that guy
because check it out:

So the bomb is ready now
and the scientists go to the president like "'Sup"
and President Truman
(who just became president
because FDR died from solving too many problems)
is like "Uhh . . . uhh . . .
fuck it, we're bombing Japan."

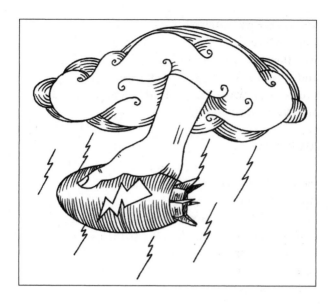

So two Japanese cities
just crawling with civilians
suddenly get vaporized
by the domesticated finger of god
and the whole world is like "Oh fuuuuuuuuuuck"
and suddenly World War Two is over
and Japan makes a ton of really weird movies
in an attempt to get over the whole thing.

Meanwhile, Russia is pissed
because Stalin is not about to let America
have a monopoly on being God
so Russia makes some nukes
and America makes some more nukes
and Britain makes some nukes
and Russia makes some more nukes
and America makes EVEN MORE NUKES
until finally everyone is like "Okay, okay.
We can all be God, it's cool.

But we have to promise
never to use these nukes on each other
because if we do
we will all stop being God really fast.
Also let's keep anyone else from getting these
because they're probably not as wise as us."

And so, once again
the gods withdrew their powers to their hidden silos
(although they're still building more)
and the world entered an era of (relative) peace
and now anytime anyone tries to challenge the gods
by making their own nukes, Prometheus-style
the U.S. totally FREAKS OUT
and buries those guys under troops and bombs
but not nuclear bombs
so it's okay.

The moral of the story
is never bring a knife to a gunfight
bring the goddamn apocalypse.

★ ★ ★

OF ALL THE PLACES ALIENS COULD HAVE VISITED, THEY CHOSE ROSWELL

Here's what the government wants you to believe:
Back in Cold War times
when the U.S. is super nervous about Russian nukes
they come up with a brilliant strategy:
duct tape some microphones to some balloons
put the balloons way up in the sky
and hope that Russia is like "Hey, balloon!
Look over here!
See all these shockwaves?
That's all our nukes!
Come sabotage them!"
They spend MILLIONS on this.

But the problem is that these million-dollar balloons
are FUCKING BALLOONS
so one day
one of these things is flying over New Mexico
and it pops
AS BALLOONS DO
and the shredded wreckage plummets to the ground
in the middle of some dude's farm
so this dude finds all this junk on his farm
like rubber, and balsa wood, and Scotch tape.
Some of the Scotch tape has flowers on it.
YUP
YOUR TAX DOLLARS AT WORK.

But not only is this balloon thing expensive
it's also MADDD SECRET
so everyone who saw the balloon go down
is like "WTF is that flying disc?"
(New Mexicans don't know what balloons are)
and all the newspapers start talking about it
until finally this farmer dude calls the sheriff
and he's like "Psst:
I think I found one of those flying discs?"

So the sheriff calls the government
and the government shows up on the farm
and is like "Oh man, thanks for finding this
dunno what we would've done
without this huge pile of useless garbage"
and they cart it away to the air force base
and presumably throw it in a dumpster, the end.

PRETTY UNLIKELY, RIGHT?
Here's what really happened:

So back in Cold War times
the U.S. is super nervous about ALIENS
because WHEN ARE THEY NOT
and then some aliens show up
joyriding their flying saucer across the galaxy
(also New Mexico)
and crash right in the middle of some dude's farm.
This is why you should never drink and drive.

This spaceship is NOT made out of trash
it is made of high-tech material
that only LOOKS like trash
also there are dead and dying aliens in the wreckage
sort of a giveaway
so the government shows up like "Hey, dude
let's just keep this between us, okay?"

and the farmer dude is like "Yeah, no worries
I'll just tell them I found a balloon or something"
and the government, being the government
is like "YES, BRILLIANT."

So they ship the aliens off to the air force base
and instead of trying to establish first contact
they skip straight to cutting them open
learning nothing useful, as far as I can tell.
Considering the dumb crap their ship's made of
there's probably not much to learn.

So the moral of the story
is that no matter how you slice it
the government is not super good at its job.

★ ★ ★

IF YOU HAVEN'T SLEPT WITH MARILYN MONROE, YOU PROBABLY AREN'T IMPORTANT

Now, if there's one thing a pantheon needs
it's a goddess of love.
The Greeks have Aphrodite
the Norse have Freya
the Christians have God
(think about how much his name gets shouted)
and Americans have
. . . blondes.

Look, the problem with using real people as gods
is that real people die
so in order to make them last a little longer
you need to make them fit big archetypes
and put a lot of makeup on them so they look similar
and pump them full of drugs and money
until they die from all the drugs
and you have to replace them.

Hollywood is amazing at this
but in order for the trick to work
they've gotta keep the archetypes pretty vague.
Therefore: the blonde.

Hollywood burns through a ton of blondes
over a ton of years
all to fulfill the public's insatiable demand

for yellow hair and nice boobs
until one day they find this young model
(hotness, check)
fresh out of a long chain of foster homes
(humble beginnings, check)
with nice blond hair
(yellow scalp-fur, check)
and her name
is Norma Jean Mortenson.

Okay, okay, cut.
Norma Jean?
Mortenson?

That shit's not gonna fly in showbiz.
So they're like "Tell ya what, toots
we'll let you keep the first letter of your last name
but everything else has gotta go.

We're gonna give you the first name of Jesus's mom
Marilyn
and the last name of a past president
who cemented U.S. neutrality
and supported Latin American independence
Monroe.
MARILYN MONROE.
It's perfect.
Okay, now put on all this makeup
and try not to be yourself."

But if Norma—ahem—Marilyn has the wrong name
and doesn't look right
and doesn't act right either
why do they want to hire her to be Queen of Sex?
Well, for the simple reason that they all have dicks
and Marilyn is SUPERNATURALLY SEXY.

For proof of this
let's look at the dudes she messed around with.
There's James Dougherty, a cop
Joe DiMaggio, a baseball star
and Arthur Miller, an award-winning playwright
and those are just the dudes she MARRIED.
You know who ELSE she slapped laps with?
JOHN F. KENNEDY
AMERICA'S SEXIEST PRESIDENT
ALSO MAYBE HIS BROTHER BOBBY
I mean, no one can exactly PROVE this
but you have got to be pretty goddamn sexy
for people to even start spreading RUMORS
that you spread your legs for the president.

She does movies too, but who cares?
I'll tell you who cares
Marilyn fucking Monroe.
She's not super stoked
at being nothing more than the latest Avatar of Blond
and getting sacrificed when her tits start to sag
so she starts hatching plans.

Her first plan is just to never get old
but that is doomed to fail
so instead she decides to get actually good at acting
so that once she's no longer pure sex incarnate
she can still get jobs doing a thing she likes.

So she gets good at acting
by taking classes and stuff
but you know what she's still not good at?
Sleeping
also, dealing with the inevitable stress
of having to be fantastic all the fucking time.
Luckily there's pills you can take for that

they're called "sleeping pills"
and what they do is
they make you sleep.
Unfortunately, Marilyn likes them too much
and she starts taking too many
and showing up later and later to stuff
until finally she doesn't show up at all
because she is the other kind of late
no, I don't mean she's pregnant
I mean she's permanently asleep, like forever.

No one is happy about this.
Marilyn Monroe was awesome
and now people are sad.
Some people say she killed herself
some people say it was an accident
and some people say it was MURDER
by like, the mafia
or the Secret Service
or Bobby Kennedy himself!
But no one gets a chance to ask Bobby about it
because some random sniper shoots him and he dies
just a little bit after the same thing happens to his bro
which is a tragedy too
although I guess
once Marilyn Monroe has sex with you
nothing is really a tragedy ever again.

The good news for Marilyn
is that she does actually manage to live forever
at least, people write books about her
and make paintings
and giant statues
where she is desperately trying
to keep her clothes from leaping off her body
and then later on
Pamela Anderson tries to cut in

and everyone is like "We see what you're trying to do
and don't get us wrong, it's really working for us
but you're never gonna touch that."

I think we can all learn a valuable lesson here
which is that it's good to be shrewd
and it's good to be pretty
and it's good to be kind or whatever
but what really matters
is banging celebrities.

Martin Luther King
Could Own You at Pool

So America has slavery
but then the Civil War happens
and slavery is over.
Yaaaaaaaaaaaay!
Except, wait
it looks like even though slavery is over
all the dudes who used to own slaves
are not very excited about enforcing these new laws
ESPECIALLY the one about black people voting
and they quickly discover a neat life hack:
Turns out that laws don't matter
if you control the police
and just straight-up kill whoever disagrees with you.

So obviously black people are not jazzed about this
and it is only a matter of time
before someone comes along to make shit better.
This someone is named Martin Luther King
and in addition to being a Doctor of Religion
(which means he fixes sick religions?)
he is also an unbelievably good speaker
dead sexy
and amazing at pool.
Also, his last name is KING.
COME ON.

With a rep like Marty's
he probably could have just been like
"Hey, everyone
wouldn't it be great if we killed all white people?"

But that's not what he's about
he's on this lame nonviolence kick
so when a badass lady named Rosa Parks
decides to get arrested on purpose
for riding the wrong part of a bus
(it is very easy to get arrested as a black person)
Marty's got her back.

Along with some other dudes
from the Southern Christian Leadership Conference
he gets everybody in Montgomery, Alabama
(where Rosa Parks got arrested)
to just not ride buses
and the bus guys are like "Oh noooo
we were getting so much money
from making black people sit in back of our buses
looks like we have to change our racist ways!"
So the bus thing gets changed, sort of
and everyone is like "Right on, Martin."
I mean, it wasn't just him who did it
but he's the sexiest one so he gets the credit.

After that, dude is in high demand
he's going all over the South
trying to make things less shitty.
Here is how he does that:
Step 1: Tell black people to march around
Step 2: Police punch all the black people
Step 3: Take pictures of the punching
Step 4: Washington's all like whaaaaat
Step 5: Justice!
This only works if police are down to punch dudes
which is not true in some places
which means Martin is unsuccessful for a bit
but then he gets to Birmingham
which is full of people who are so terrible
it is essentially a village of tiny redneck Hitlers.

So King gets thrown in jail by these mega racists
and a ton of well-meaning white people up north
are like "Whoa, dude, maybe chill out a bit."
so he writes them a letter like "Dear white people
you seem to think I should chill out
but it is hard as hell to chill out
when dudes are throwing rocks at your head
for not being the same color as their head.
If I wait any longer to stop all these rocks
the rocks are going to hit me in the head
and it won't even matter what color my head is
because I will be dead.
P.S.: You guys are totally not helping."
And everyone is like "Oh, wow, good point."

But while he's in jail
people are still protesting in Birmingham
and it's not really working
because pretty much all the protesters are in jail.
But you know who's not in jail?
LITTLE CHILDREN.
So this one dude gets on the radio
like "HEY KIDS
YOU KNOW WHAT'S GREAT?
MORTAL DANGER."
And the next day
the streets are full of black toddlers
waving signs and adorably risking their lives.
And what do the police do?
ARREST THEM.
They arrest like a thousand little kids.
They put them in JAIL
then when they run out of toddlers to arrest
they sic vicious dogs on high school students
while blasting them with high-pressure hoses.
I'm pretty sure that if there were babies to punt
the cops probably would have done that too.

At this point the government is like "Okay, okay
the level of evil on display here would be hilarious
if this were not A REAL THING
THAT YOU ARE ACTUALLY DOING.
STOP IT."
So they send in the National Guard
and President John F. Kennedy
who up to this point has been too busy getting laid
to worry about civil rights
is finally like "Jeez, fine
I will try to make some laws to help with this shit."

But whereas JFK moves fast with the ladies
he moves hella slow with groundbreaking legislation
so Martin finally shows up at his house
(by which I mean Washington, DC)
with two hundred thousand other people
and they camp out in front of a big statue
of that Abraham Lincoln guy
who supposedly freed all the slaves
and King is like "Guys, I had this crazy dream
where white people and black people
didn't hate the shit out of each other
wow, so crazy!
P.S.: JFK could you hurry up on that law please?"

But JFK has bigger fish to fry
namely the big red fish of COMMUNISM
and it doesn't help that the head of the FBI
(J. Edgar Hoover
who got his last name by sucking real hard)
HATES black people
. . . I mean he hates Martin Luther King.
No way is Hoover a racist. No no no.
So Hoover is trying to tell JFK that King's a commie
but then he gives up
and just starts trying to prove that he's a pervert

which is WAY easier
'cause everywhere King goes
he swings dick like an erotic grandfather clock
his core philosophy is "I'm a married Baptist minister
but like
whatever."
So Hoover records all of King's sex parties
and sends the tapes to King's wife
which makes everyone sad
so great job, J. Edgar Suckpants.

Then Kennedy gets shot
nobody knows why
maybe they were jealous of how laid he was getting
but regardless, the new president is Lyndon Johnson
who is from Texas
so everyone gets ready for some executive racism
but Johnson surprises the shit out of everyone
by ramming that civil rights bill through Congress.
Then he decides he's made enough good decisions
and invades Vietnam.

Now, Martin Luther King's whole MO is nonviolence
he is always the dude at the protest
who keeps his dudes from throwing punches
even when the other guys are throwing bullets
so he hears about this Vietnam business
and he is like "Oh HELL no"
and Lyndon B. Johnson is like "God dammit, Marty
I thought we were friends"
and Eddie Hoover is like "Hey, Lyndon
have I played these MLK sex tapes for you yet?
Pretty sure that dude's a SEX COMMUNIST"
and LBJ is like "AAAAAAH MARTY!"

But Martin Luther King keeps protesting the war
even when his friends are like "Dude, chill out

we still need to solve racism."
He even starts saying some really problematic stuff
about how his REAL goal is to end poverty
so now he has made enemies of racists, war hawks
AND rich dudes
which is why
when he is mysteriously shot in Memphis, Tennessee
at the age of thirty-nine
everybody is sad
but nobody is surprised.

Everybody is so sad
that pretty much every city in the United States
catches on fire for like a week
and then they name a bunch of streets after him
and celebrate his birthday so hard
that no one has to go to school on it
EVER AGAIN.
But at least racism is over!
. . . right?

So basically
be careful never to be too awesome
or you will be mysteriously executed
just like Martin Luther King
and Gandhi
and Abraham Lincoln
and JFK
and Malcolm X
and Sitting Bull
and Crazy Horse
and . . . wow
why are we so mean to our best people?

KENNEDY TRIES
TO NUKE THE MOON

All right kiddies, I've got one more for ya
but it spans hecka time
so we've gotta jump back to World War Two for a sec
because that's when we nuked all our old gods.
Check it:

So Germany is having a war with everyone
like I said
and one of the things they do
is they hire this dude named Von Braun
to build them some rockets
so Von Braun, who is an awesome engineer
is like "Sweet
we can use these rockets to go to space!
Hey . . . wait
why are you pointing my rockets at other countries?
ohhh, I get it.
Well, fuck you too, Hitler."

But then Hitler loses the war by being a crazy person
and the U.S. captures Von Braun and some of his bros
and Von Braun is like "Sweet!
Now I can finally build rockets to go to space!
Wait . . . guys?
Why are you pointing my rockets at Russia?
OH, FUCK YOU GUYS.
SERIOUSLY, WHAT THE HELL."

Now, to be fair to the United States
Russia is a big, scary country

with their own stolen German scientists
and their own nuclear weapons
and their own economic system.
But to be fair to Russia
the United States is a big, scary country
that has already nuked one country it didn't like
and is now using a bunch of stolen German scientists
to point bigger and bigger nuclear missiles at Russia
soooo . . .
everybody goes a little crazy for a while
Resulting in something called the Cold War.
I don't know why it's so cold
like, nobody ever called any of the other wars "hot"
but I guess every war against Russia is pretty cold
so there you go.

So Russia and the U.S. spend several years
pointing larger and larger missiles at each other
until dudes in both countries are suddenly like
"Wait a second
these missiles we're building are HUGE
I bet they're big enough to go to SPACE"
and Von Braun is just like "YEAH NO SHIT."

So Khrushchev, who is the head of Russia
and Eisenhower, who is the head of the United States
both decide that the best way to win the Cold War
is to be the first country to put dudes in space
and then just be so cool as a result of that
that their enemies automatically bow down to them.
Oh, okay, I get it
THAT'S why it's called the Cold War.
Cool War probably would have been better
but I guess we all make mistakes.

For the next four years
Russia hands the United States its ass over and over.

They launch the first satellite
(which is basically just a big metal ball that beeps)
and the U.S. responds
by blowing up a rocket on the launchpad
on national TV.
So to make up for that embarrassment
they train a bunch of astronauts
(meaning "star-voyagers")
and start a cutting edge program
code-named "Man in Space Soonest"
(seriously)
but the Russians beat them to that too
with their team of COSMOnauts
(meaning "UNIVERSE-voyagers")
until finally Eisenhower stops being president
and JFK takes over
and he's like "Eisenhower was a douche bag
he gave our space program to a nonmilitary group
(suck it, NASA)
and he spent billions on it.
But I'm an even bigger douche bag than he
because I am going to take our space program
TO THE MOON
LITERALLY.
The Russians are schooling us so hard
our only hope is to pick a goal no one can achieve
and then hope all the Russian scientists die
before they can beat us to it.
We will do this incredibly stupid thing
not because it is easy
but for the same reason we play football:
That is to say
basically no reason at all."

Then Kennedy hedges his bets
by trying to make a deal with Khrushchev
to work TOGETHER on this moon shit

but BOOM, HEADSHOT
Kennedy dies, and LBJ takes over
and Khrushchev doesn't like LBJ
so SPACE RACE AHOY.

The U.S. starts the Apollo program
which should be called the Artemis program
because Apollo is the god of the sun
and Artemis is in charge of the moon
and also his sister
but at this time dudes are pretty sure ladies can't math
so yayyyy 1960s.

Anyway, for nine years after that
the U.S. and the USSR take turns
flinging their best and brightest into space
(or in Russia's case, just whoever they can find
like a dog
or a bag of turtles
or even A WOMAN)
and eventually JFK's wildest dreams come true
because Sergei Korolev
who has basically been handling all Russia's science
decides to die
and the scientists Russia has left
apparently learned how to make spaceships
from that old silent film *A Trip to the Moon*
where the moon is a guy's face covered in cheese
and they fire a rocket out of a cannon into his eye.
So they just keep failing
while the U.S. is firing dudes ever closer to the moon.

Finally, on the ELEVENTH TRY
the U.S. gets a big shuttle into space
named after the jerk who "discovered" America
and it has a lunar module on it
with a lander, and a couple of guys

but then everybody gets impatient
and they're like "Okay, y'all
[they're in Houston, btw]
we've spent billions and billions of dollars
cooked human beings to death inside space coffins
and done WAY MORE MATH than is okay
but you know what?
Landing on the moon seems real hard.
Let's just not and say we did."
So they film the moon landing on Earth.
Stanley Kubrick directs it, it's great
and they get this actor named Neil Armstrong
to stride out of the lander all majestic
like "Hey, this one tiny step I'm taking?
This is like a HUGE leap for mankind
mostly because gravity is way lower up here.
Look, I can jump SO HIGH. WHOA."

Neil Armstrong pretty much becomes a god after that
because think about it
the moon is a thing people used to WORSHIP.
Like, the best heroes of ancient Greece
dreamed of being turned into star pictures at death
just so they could chill with the fucking moon
and this dude
just walked on her FACE.
(Uh, I mean
on a sound stage that LOOKS like her face.
THE TRUTH IS OUT THERE.)

It's hard to compete with that
so pretty soon after the moon landing
Russia is like "Okay, fuck it"
and stops trying to put dudes on the moon
because seriously, who needs dudes on the moon?
The U.S. also stops trying very hard
because science just isn't as fun

when there's no one to humiliate.
Instead, they all start building cool space forts
and President Nixon makes a deal with Russia
where both countries send a ship to space
and then they link up in orbit
and the astronauts hang out
thus making the U.S. and Russia the first nations
ever to HIGH-FIVE IN SPACE.
THAT, MY FRIENDS
IS THE HIGHEST OF FIVES.

Then they sign a treaty
that says you can't use the moon for military stuff
thus ensuring
that no one will ever give enough of a shit
to try and go to the moon ever again
so great job, assholes.

And since then, the world has been at peace
except for all the guerilla wars
and terrorism
and gang violence and covert ops
and random shelling across national borders
and arms races and air strikes
and the death penalty and *American Gladiators*
but that's just what we like to call
"the spice of life."

The lesson here
is that war is never the answer
unless the question is
"How do you get to the moon?"

CONCLUSION

A Myth in Progress

So if you're reading this, you've probably read my book. Maybe you haven't, but I don't know what kind of person skips to the conclusion of a hilarious book of myths. Go back and read some stories, and then we can talk.

Okay, we good?

Good.

Writing this book has been a challenge, because when it comes to the United States, the mythology is still very much jumbled together with the history. Nobody gives a shit what year Zeus turned into a swan and fucked Leda, but most of the stories we tell each other in the USA fit together into a larger story, a story that's still getting written, about some crazy idiots who decided to make a government based on equal representation and just a *little* bit of slavery (coincidentally, the Greeks tried to do the same thing, and the stories of how that worked out are equally hilarious).

So not only did I need to research all these stories and relate them to you in my dumb voice, I needed to actually convince you guys that the history of the United States of America *is* its mythology. I hope I've managed that. If not, here are some things to consider:

Time and time again, historical people have used

213

mythological people to make themselves look better. Just looking at the civil rights movement—we've got Harriet Tubman nicknamed Moses, Frederick Douglass comparing himself to Jesus in his autobiography, and Martin Luther King wrapping his entire message in the sweet, sweet rhetoric of the Christian Bible.

If you look closely, you can see past presidents of the United States getting used the same way. During the 2008 presidential election, Barack Obama was compared to both JFK and Lincoln, two revered presidents, both of whom achieved godlike status by dying in office. These guys weren't just shot, they were *martyred*. The difference between death and martyrdom? Pure mythology.

And what about monuments? Every significant person in our history has a big pile of rocks dedicated to them. Four of the presidents mentioned in this book have their faces carved into a frikkin' mountain. (A mountain sacred to the Native Americans, though that kind of disrespect probably shouldn't surprise you at this point.) Of the four dudes on that mountain, Abraham Lincoln has another statue that looks a hell of a lot like the statue of Zeus at Olympia, George Washington has a big stone dick—I mean *obelisk*—right around the corner, the Jefferson Memorial looks like the goddamn Parthenon, and all four of these bastards are on our money.

Elvis's house is a pilgrimage site. So is Michael Jackson's. We built an obelisk on the site of Custer's Last Stand, and dug a hole where the Twin Towers fell. Because yeah, that's mythology too. Or it will be, once we've had time to digest it.

Actually, this book originally contained a retelling of the story of September 11, in full detail. It talked about the violence, and the heroism, and the mass hysteria that followed. My publisher convinced me to take it out. Why? Because not enough time has passed since that day. Some people are over it, but some people will take lifetimes to heal, and mythology can't happen until everybody has moved on. I guarantee you that fourteen years after Honest Abe's death, nobody was about to publish *Abraham Lincoln: Vampire Hunter*.

But the healing process has already begun. A couple days after the attack, Jon Stewart made a speech on *The Daily Show*. He was crying, he was deeply moved, he wasn't ready to make jokes about the whole thing. But he said something important. I mean, he said a lot of important things that day, and if you haven't seen that speech then you should put this book down right now and go find it, but one of the things he said was this:

"One of my first memories is of Martin Luther King being shot. I was five. Here's what I remember about it: I was in a school in Trenton, and they shut the lights off and we got to sit under our desks, and we thought that was really cool, and they gave us cottage cheese. Which was a cold lunch, because there was rioting, but we didn't know that, we just thought 'My god, we get to sit under our desks and eat cottage cheese.'"

And people laughed when he said that. Because it was proof of how we heal from these things. We get far enough away to forget a little. We make jokes. We tell and retell the stories to each other, until the memory is replaced by the story. That's how myths are made.

In 2011, President Barack Obama, heir to the ghosts of Abe Lincoln and John Kennedy, ordered the death of Osama Bin Laden. Bin Laden wasn't doing a lot of terrorist shit at the time. He was holed up in Iran with about a terabyte of American porn, trying desperately not to be killed. The point of the assassination wasn't to end Bin Laden's threat to Freedom. It was to give us an end to a terrible story.

I'm calling it now: In two thousand years, when our descendants are living in Alpha Centauri and New York is a mythical place like Atlantis or Valhalla, September 11 will be a full-blown myth. Bin Laden will become an avatar of the Devil. The people of flight 93 will be Valkyries. And George Bush will still be an idiot. But that's okay, because myths are full of those.

The point of studying mythology, to me, is to make us aware of how the patterns of mythology show up in our everyday lives. Being able to regurgitate the ridiculous sexploits of the ancient gods is a fun party trick, but the real trick is being able to spot a new myth as it's being born. September 11 is the best example we have of a myth in progress, and we all have the power to shape how it ends up being told.

In just over a decade, that story has already been used by the government to justify two invasions and an assassination. It's been used by truthers to justify hating the government. It's been used by pundits and politicians to highlight the virtues of the American people. It's been used by people, individuals who have told their personal stories in comic books and on podcasts, in bars and in chat rooms. Mythology, like this country, is sort of democratic that way.

When the planes hit, I was twelve years old, in a bathtub in California. It didn't seem real to me at the time, which I guess gave me a head start mythology-wise. Now, double the age I was in that bathtub, I just hope I get to live long enough to see the story-making process through. If I don't, though, I'm not worried. As long as there are humans, there will be bards.

ACKNOWLEDGMENTS

It's sort of tempting to just thank every person who did any kind of nice thing for me during the months I was writing this book, because writing a book tends to take over my life to the point where everything that happens seems like a part of it, but that would be boring and I would definitely forget somebody and then they'd get mad at me and it would just be a whole thing. So instead, I'm just gonna say a couple precision thank-yous and be done.

This book would have been impossible to write if Chicago didn't have such a rad public library system. Seriously, there are buildings where you can just walk in and they will GIVE YOU BOOKS. One thing I learned in reading about early American history is that the most influential people were the ones who managed to get their paws on the most books. Knowledge used to be crazy hard to get back in the day, and that gives me a new appreciation for this city's abundant free book houses.

I am indebted, as always, to my parents, Laurie O'Brien and Carl Weintraub, not only for creating me with some kind of gross sex ritual, but for being startlingly impartial proofreaders. Kristin Mann, my wonderful girlfriend, gave me time to work, bolstered my confidence with hers, and offered some key insights. Meg Leder, Amanda Shih, and the rest of the crew at Perigee transformed my napkin scribblings into something legible to other humans, and for that I am grateful. And without the intervention of Agent Extraordinaire Brandi Bowles at Foundry Literary Media, I would probably be living in a cardboard box, so there's that.

Shout-out to my Chicago family—the BYOT bastards, and the Ink and Blood collective, for making this city livable, even in winter. Also Philosophy Bro and the Cards Against Humanity people for letting me squat in their office while I worked on this. This book was written on an ASUS X200MA, which you should never buy because I'm pretty sure the keyboard is designed to maximize typos, and it has just slightly more processing power than oatmeal. It was hella cheap, though.

And of course, all praise to Tiresias Chang, without whose prodding five years ago, none of you would be reading any of this crap.

FURTHER READING

So while I was writing this book, I read some other books in order to make my book more legit, and increase my American history cred. Some of these books aren't great—I mainly just went to the appropriate shelf at the library and grabbed books with pretty spines—but in the interest of completeness and knowledge and whatever, here they all are:

American Heroes: Profiles of Men and Women Who Shaped Early America, by Edmund S. Morgan, is probably the dopest piece of history I read for this project. It's a collection of well-researched essays that questions popular opinions about the Founders without just bashing on them the way a lot of pop history tends to.

Autobiography, and Other Writings, by Benjamin Franklin, edited by Ormond Seavey, is obviously something I had to read. Ben's writing shaped early America, and autobiographies in general are great from a mythological perspective because dudes like to make themselves look SO GOOD.

Thomas Jefferson: Author of America, by Christopher Hitchens, is a pretty well-balanced account, which highlights Jefferson's accomplishments while kind of making him look like a little punk.

Why Sacagawea Deserves a Day Off, and Other Lessons from the Lewis and Clark Trail, by Stephanie Ambrose Tubbs, reads more like a personal travelogue sometimes, but raises some interesting points about the details of the expedition. A great supplement to a wider understanding of the trail.

We Shall Remain: America Through Native Eyes isn't a book. It's a great PBS series that covers a lot more Native American history than what I touched on in this book.

Harriet Tubman: Leading the Way to Freedom, by Lauri Calkhoven, is a biography for kids, rife with popular misconceptions and oversimplifications. Which is sort of perfect for me, honestly, because I'm just as interested in the stuff we make up about our heroes as I am in the facts.

Abraham Lincoln, by James M. McPherson, is a straight-up, no-nonsense overview of Lincoln's life. In under a hundred pages, McPherson packs in a lot of info, making a pretty good case for Lincoln's sometimes questionable decisions.

Behind Enemy Lines: The Incredible Story of Emma Edmonds, Civil War Spy, by Seymour Reit, is another children's biography, this one written as a prose novel. It's very well researched, though, and since Edmonds's autobiography is out of print and difficult to find, children's books are unfortunately the main place her story survives.

Bloodshed at Little Bighorn: Sitting Bull, Custer, and the Destinies of Nations, by Tim Lehman, is a really excellent account of the events leading up to Custer's Last

Stand—the politics, the military maneuvers, and the unavoidable tragedy of the whole thing.

Not for Ourselves Alone: The Story of Elizabeth Cady Stanton and Susan B. Anthony is a two-part PBS miniseries that does a great job of contrasting Anthony's pragmatism with Stanton's radical idealism, while also highlighting their lasting friendship and the salient points of the larger suffrage movement.

Capone: The Life and World of Al Capone, by John Kobler, is one of my new favorite books. Kobler goes on wild, fascinating tangents about all the minor characters in 1920s gangland, and the rippling coincidences that tie them back to Capone himself.

Lords of Finance: The Bankers Who Broke the World, by Liaquat Ahamed, is not as anticapitalist as the title makes it sound. Ahamed is an unapologetic Keynesian in his analysis of what caused the Great Depression, and he makes a damn good case for his interpretation. The little anecdotes about the Central Bankers are fascinating too. I wish I'd been able to sneak some into this book.

At Issue in History: Japanese American Internment Camps, edited by William Dudley, is how I believe all history should be taught. It's a well-curated collection of primary and secondary sources on the issue, with all viewpoints carefully represented. Still, it's hard not to come out of it feeling like the United States goofed.

The Manhattan Project: A Documentary Introduction to the Atomic Age, by R. Hal Williams, Jonathan F. Fanton, and Michael F. Stoff, takes the collection-of-sources angle even farther by telling the whole story of the atom bomb through reproductions of official top-secret documents. It's dense as hell, but it's also really funny to see Truman being totally passive-aggressive to the secretary of war, and stuff like that.

Martin Luther King, by Godfrey Hodgson, was actually pretty hard to read. What's cool about it is that Hodgson was a reporter at the time of the civil rights movement, so he got to interview King and all that. What's bad about it is that the book isn't very well edited. The chronology is hard to follow, and typos abound.

Conversations with Marilyn, by William J. Weatherby, is a touching story that offers some good insight into Monroe, but it definitely seems like Weatherby played up his connection with her for the sake of publicity. Dude saw her, what, four times?

ABOUT THE AUTHOR

Cory O'Brien is a storyteller by trade, but has also worked as a dishwasher, a plumber's apprentice, a political canvasser, and a street juggler. He lives in Chicago, where he fills his time by doing twenty-four-hour plays and working in a woodshop on Tuesdays. He has an MFA in writing from the School of the Art Institute of Chicago. Birds terrify him more than anything. They're highly mobile sociopaths with beady eyes and hollow bones, come on.